3 THE HARD WAY

How Allen Iverson Reshaped The Culture

Miles Truman

HHV Publishing

Copyright

This book is an independent, unauthorized documentary work of journalism.

It is not endorsed, authorized, or approved by Allen Iverson, the NBA, the Philadelphia 76ers, or any related entity.

For information, inquiries, or permissions, contact:
HHV Publishing

ISBN: 978-1-970850-00-0
Printed in the United States of America
First Edition: 2025

Table of Contents

Introduction (When The Culture Changed)

It was March 12, 1997, in the dim glow of Chicago's United Center, when a rookie named Allen Iverson, barely 21 and sporting a fresh set of cornrows that defied the NBA's polished image, dribbled the ball with an audacity that bordered on heresy. Facing Michael Jordan, the god of basketball, Iverson executed a crossover dribble so sharp it left Jordan stumbling, his Airness reduced to a mere mortal for a split second. Iverson pulled up and drained the jumper, the crowd erupting in a mix of shock and awe. This wasn't just a highlight-reel play; it was a seismic shift. Iverson, the undersized guard from Hampton, Virginia, with a backstory laced in poverty, incarceration, and raw survival, had arrived not as an heir to Jordan's throne but as its disruptor. In that moment, the culture of basketball cracked open. The league, long dominated by clean-cut icons and corporate appeal, felt the intrusion of something street-born, unapologetic, and profoundly Black. Iverson didn't just beat Jordan; he signaled the end of an era where assimilation was the price of entry. His presence injected an authenticity that resonated beyond the court, pulling in fans who saw themselves in his defiance. This crossover wasn't merely athletic—it was cultural, marking the point when hip-hop's rhythm began syncing with the squeak of sneakers, when tattoos and baggy shorts became symbols of rebellion rather than deviance. The NBA, once a bastion of conformity, was forever altered by a 6-foot phenom who played like he had nothing to lose because, in truth, he had already lost so much.

Iverson's reshaping of identity in the NBA started with his body, a canvas of ink and braids that challenged the league's aesthetic norms. Tattoos, once whispered about in locker rooms as markers of thuggery, became badges of honor under his influence. His cornrows, inspired by the streets of his youth, weren't just a hairstyle; they were a declaration of cultural pride, echoing the styles of rappers like Tupac and Snoop Dogg. Players before him had flirted with edge—Dennis Rodman with his dyed hair and piercings—but Iverson made it mainstream, authentic, and inseparable from excellence. He averaged 26 points as a rookie, proving that style and substance could coexist, even thrive. This authenticity extended to his demeanor: no forced smiles for cameras, no scripted press conferences. Iverson spoke in the vernacular of his upbringing, raw and unfiltered, alienating some while magnetizing others. He embodied the "keep it real" ethos of 90s hip-hop, where vulnerability about struggles—his mother's sacrifices, his own brushes with the law—humanized the superstar. In a league pushing for global marketability, Iverson's identity forced a reckoning: Could basketball embrace players who refused to sand down their edges? His answer was a resounding yes, paving the way for future generations to enter the NBA as their full selves, not diluted versions tailored for endorsement deals. This shift wasn't superficial; it redefined what it meant to be a baller, blending athletic prowess with cultural narrative in ways that made the game more inclusive, more reflective of America's diverse undercurrents.

Yet, Iverson's impact on aesthetics went deeper, transforming the visual language of the sport. Baggy jerseys, arm sleeves, and crossover chains became his uniform, imported straight from urban fashion scenes. Before him, NBA style leaned toward tailored suits and conservative cuts, a holdover from the Bird-Magic era. Iverson flipped the script, drawing from hip-hop's oversized silhouettes and bold accessories, making the court a runway for streetwear. His Reebok sneakers, the Question and Answer lines, sold out not just for performance but for their cultural cachet, blending athletic tech with rap-inspired designs. This aesthetic revolution sparked backlash—commissioner David Stern's infamous dress code in 2005 was a direct response to Iverson's influence, aiming to curb what he saw as "hip-hop" encroachment. But Iverson's look wasn't rebellion for its own sake; it was an extension of his authenticity, a visual manifesto of Black expression in a white-dominated industry. Fans, especially young Black kids, saw in him a mirror: someone who looked like them, dressed like them, and succeeded on his terms. This aesthetic shift democratized basketball's image, making it accessible to those outside suburban gyms. It influenced designers like Virgil Abloh and brands like Nike, who later embraced street culture in their lines. Iverson didn't just change how players dressed; he altered how the world perceived basketball's beauty, turning grit into glamour and proving that aesthetics born from the margins could redefine the center.

The intersections of Iverson's world with hip-hop were inevitable, electric, and transformative. Growing up in the era of Biggie and Jay-Z, Iverson didn't just listen to rap—he lived it. His friendships with artists like Jadakiss and DMX weren't PR stunts; they were organic bonds forged in shared struggles of inner-city life. Iverson appeared in music videos, rapped on tracks, and even released his own album under the moniker "Jewelz," blurring the lines between athlete and entertainer. This synergy amplified his icon status: hip-hop provided the soundtrack to his crossovers, his trash-talk echoing the bravado of battle raps. In turn, Iverson brought basketball into rap's lexicon, with lyrics referencing his speed, his heart, his unyielding spirit. Fashion followed suit—his cornrows inspired a wave in hip-hop style, while his tattoos influenced album art and streetwear trends. Cultural expression flourished in this crossover: Iverson's "practice" rant in 2002, a raw outpouring of frustration, became a meme, a mantra, sampled in songs and etched into pop culture. This fusion wasn't superficial; it highlighted how both worlds grappled with authenticity amid commercialization. Hip-hop's rise paralleled the NBA's global expansion, and Iverson was the bridge, showing how cultural expression could elevate both. His presence made basketball cooler, more rhythmic, infusing the game with hip-hop's narrative depth—stories of triumph over adversity that resonated across demographics.

Beyond style and sound, Iverson's fashion influence reshaped broader cultural expression in sports. He turned accessories into statements: the shooting sleeve he popularized for practical reasons became a staple, symbolizing resilience. His disdain for suits—opting for throwback jerseys and durags at events—challenged the NBA's performative professionalism, sparking debates on race and respectability. This wasn't mere fashion; it was a form of resistance, asserting that Black cultural aesthetics deserved space in elite arenas. Iverson's impact rippled into streetwear empires, influencing brands like Supreme and Off-White, which drew from his blend of athletic and urban vibes. In a league increasingly commodified, his authenticity preserved cultural integrity, reminding players that expression could be both personal and profitable. This intersection empowered athletes to leverage their platforms, turning endorsements into extensions of identity rather than erasures. Iverson's era marked when fashion became a battlefield for cultural agency, where what you wore spoke volumes about where you came from. Today, stars like LeBron James and Russell Westbrook owe their stylistic freedom to Iverson's trailblazing, proving that cultural expression isn't accessory—it's essential to the game's evolution.

Iverson's presence shifted the NBA fundamentally, forcing the league to confront its biases and adapt to a changing demographic. His 2001 MVP season, leading the underdog 76ers to the Finals, wasn't just about stats—31 points per game, steals leader—it was a narrative coup. Stepping over Ty Lue after a bucket in Game 1 symbolized dominance over the establishment, the Lakers representing the old guard. Stern's dress code, while controversial, acknowledged Iverson's power: the league couldn't ignore the cultural wave he unleashed. Ratings soared with his antics, drawing urban audiences previously alienated by the sport's elitism. This shift diversified the fanbase, making basketball a global cultural export infused with American street ethos. Iverson's defiance exposed hypocrisies—why celebrate Jordan's competitiveness but vilify Iverson's? His impact humanized the game, showing vulnerability as strength. The league's pivot toward player empowerment, from mental health discussions to social justice stances, traces back to his unfiltered honesty. Iverson didn't just play; he redefined success, proving that icons could emerge from the fringes, reshaping the NBA into a more inclusive, expressive arena.

Why does Iverson's impact matter today? In an era of polished superteams and social media personas, his raw authenticity serves as a reminder of basketball's roots in struggle and self-expression. Modern players like Ja Morant or Kyrie Irving channel his flair, but Iverson's blueprint endures amid debates on athlete activism and identity. His story underscores how cultural icons bridge divides, influencing everything from sneaker culture to racial discourse in sports. As the NBA grapples with globalization, Iverson's legacy highlights the value of unapologetic Black excellence, inspiring youth to embrace their heritage. In a world quick to commodify rebellion, his journey matters because it proves culture isn't static—it's shaped by those bold enough to change it.

Origins of a Phenom

In the shadow of the Chesapeake Bay, Hampton, Virginia, sprawled like a fractured mosaic in the 1980s and early 1990s—a city etched by the ghosts of its past as a primary port for enslaved Africans arriving on American shores. Here, in this Tidewater hub of shipyards and military bases, racial lines carved deep divides, with Black and white residents inhabiting parallel worlds. Neighborhoods like Aberdeen, where young Allen Iverson navigated his formative years, pulsed with the raw energy of survival amid poverty's grip. Sewage sometimes flooded streets, homes lacked basic stability, and single mothers like Iverson's own—barely out of childhood herself at 15 when he was born—juggled multiple jobs, leaving kids to fend for themselves in a landscape riddled with temptation.

Violence simmered as a constant undercurrent: gunshots echoed through the night, gang influences lured the vulnerable, and children as young as 12 huddled by dumpsters, inhaling cocaine in broad daylight. The social fabric frayed along economic fault lines, where hope often evaporated in the haze of drugs and despair. Yet, amid this crucible, community identity coalesced around resilience and pride, particularly in the Black enclaves where family ties and street bonds forged unbreakable loyalties. Sports reigned supreme, a beacon in the chaos—high school football fields and basketball courts transformed into arenas of redemption. For young athletes, the pressure was immense: excel or succumb. Talent like Iverson's, honed on cracked asphalt and fueled by dreams of escape, became a lifeline, channeling raw aggression into glory. Coaches and mentors preached discipline, but the streets taught survival, molding phenoms who carried the weight of their hometown's struggles on every crossover dribble. In Hampton, potential bloomed not despite the hardship, but because of it—a testament to the unyielding spirit that propelled one boy from the projects toward immortality.

In the cramped confines of a modest apartment in Aberdeen Gardens, Allen Iverson's world revolved around a matriarch whose grit mirrored the city's own. Ann Iverson, just fifteen when she gave birth to Allen on June 7, 1975, embodied the fierce determination of a young Black mother thrust into adulthood overnight. With Allen's biological father, Allen Broughton, largely absent and later imprisoned on drug charges, Ann shouldered the burden alone until she met Michael Freeman, who became a stepfather figure but brought his own demons—heroin addiction and dealing that invited chaos into their home. The household swelled with siblings: younger sisters Brandy and Iiesha, and later a brother, Mister Allen, creating a volatile mix of love and instability where police raids and overdoses were as routine as meals.

Economic strife gnawed at every corner. Welfare checks stretched thin, utilities flickered on and off, and food stamps dictated survival. Ann worked tirelessly—cleaning jobs, waitressing—often leaving Allen, the eldest, to assume parental roles by age ten. He changed diapers, cooked simple meals from scant pantries, and shielded his siblings from the neighborhood's predators, all while dodging the allure of quick money from street hustles. These early responsibilities forged a steel-trap mentality: trust no one fully, fight for every inch, and turn vulnerability into armor. Iverson's survival instincts sharpened like a blade—learning to read intentions in a glance, to pivot from danger with the same agility he'd later display on the court. The constant pressure bred a defiance, a refusal to be defined by circumstance, planting the seeds of a warrior ethos that would define his path. Yet, beneath the bravado, a deep loyalty to family anchored him, transforming hardship into the fuel for his unyielding drive.

In the dim glow of intermittent streetlights, Allen Iverson's early life unfolded as a relentless storm of instability, where emotional scars ran as deep as the cracks in the pavement. Poverty wasn't just a backdrop; it was a predator, lurking in busted pipes that flooded homes with sewage, forcing choices between electricity and a meager meal. Ann's unyielding hustle couldn't shield her son from the chaos—police raids shattered any illusion of safety, and the arrest of Michael Freeman at age 13 etched betrayal into young Allen's psyche, compelling him to repeat eighth grade amid the fallout. Surrounded by death's shadow—friends lost to drugs and violence—he learned early that vulnerability was a luxury he couldn't afford, masking fear with a defiant glare that became his armor.

Expectations weighed heavy, too. As the eldest, dubbed "Bubba Chuck" for his protective instincts over neighborhood kids, Iverson internalized a leader's burden: provide, protect, prevail. Yet, the community's dual edges cut both ways—mentors like AAU coach Boo Williams ignited hope through sports, channeling rage into triumphs on the court and field, while street temptations and racial tensions exploded in the 1993 bowling alley brawl. Convicted amid controversy, his four months in prison forged an unbreakable resolve, refusing to cry or crumble, emerging with an identity steeped in resilience. This crucible of hardship—blending familial fractures, societal pressures, and raw survival—sculpted a phenom who viewed the world through a lens of unapologetic authenticity, turning pain into the fire that propelled him beyond Hampton's grasp.

On the cracked fields and worn courts of Bethel High School, Allen Iverson's athletic gifts erupted like a force of nature, defying the odds in a region where specialization was the norm. By his sophomore year, Iverson had already commandeered the football team as a dynamic quarterback, slinging passes with pinpoint accuracy and eluding defenders with a slippery elusiveness that left opponents grasping at air. In 1991, he tied a Virginia state record with five interceptions in a single game, anchoring a defense that propelled Bethel to an undefeated regular season. But it was his junior year that cemented his legend: leading the Bruins to the 1992 Group AAA state football championship, Iverson dazzled as a dual-threat QB, rushing for over 1,000 yards while throwing for touchdowns that electrified crowds. Mere months later, he pivoted to basketball, averaging 31 points per game and guiding Bethel to the 1993 state title with crossover dribbles and no-look passes that seemed otherworldly.

This dual-sport supremacy was extraordinary—few athletes, let alone in Virginia's competitive high school ranks, dominated two disciplines so thoroughly, blending football's brute physicality with basketball's finesse. Coaches like Mike Bailey in football and Dennis Kozlowski in basketball marveled at his raw talent, often pulling him from one practice to another, dubbing him a "once-in-a-generation" phenom whose work ethic matched his flair. Peers whispered in awe, nicknaming him "The Answer" for his ability to solve any on-field riddle, while fostering a mix of envy and inspiration in locker rooms. Local media, from the Daily Press to WAVY-TV, chronicled his exploits with front-page fervor, hailing him as Hampton's hometown hero whose feats offered a rare escape from the area's socioeconomic woes. Yet, this spotlight amplified the pressures, turning every game into a high-stakes audition for a future beyond the streets.

In the blistering heat of Virginia's autumn Fridays, Allen Iverson transformed Bethel High School's football field into his personal coliseum, where speed and ferocity collided in a symphony of dominance. As quarterback, safety, and kick returner, Iverson's multifaceted role showcased a rare blend of athleticism: a cannon arm that rifled passes through defenses, legs that blurred like shadows evading tackles, and a vision that anticipated plays before they unfolded. His junior year pinnacle came in 1992, quarterbacking the Bruins to a flawless 14-0 season and the Group AAA Division 5 state championship. In the title game against E.C. Glass, Iverson accounted for over 200 yards of offense, including a game-sealing touchdown run that left defenders sprawled in his wake. But it was his defensive prowess—snaring interceptions with predatory instinct and delivering bone-jarring hits—that amplified his legend, earning him the Associated Press Player of the Year honors.

Iverson's intensity burned like an unquenchable fire; he played with a reckless abandon, diving headfirst into piles, absorbing punishment that would sideline lesser athletes. This wasn't mere bravado—it was leadership incarnate. Teammates rallied around his unyielding spirit, inspired by pep talks laced with street wisdom and a refusal to accept defeat. "Bubba Chuck" led not by decree but by example, pushing practices to exhaustion and fostering a brotherhood that mirrored his protective family instincts. Local legends whispered of his exploits: crowds swelling to capacity, scouts from powerhouses like Florida State and Notre

Dame scribbling notes in awe. Football's brutal physicality honed his toughness, teaching him to rise from every hit, channeling pain into power—a resilience that would later define his NBA battles. In Hampton, Iverson wasn't just a player; he was the embodiment of defiance, a local icon whose gridiron glory etched his name into Tidewater lore.

Amid the echoing squeaks of sneakers on Bethel High's gymnasium floor, Allen Iverson's reputation as a basketball virtuoso solidified, a blur of motion that left defenders bewildered and crowds electrified. Standing at just 6 feet—undersized for a guard in an era dominated by towering athletes—Iverson shattered preconceptions with a game built on blistering speed, improvisational creativity, and an audacious fearlessness that bordered on the supernatural. His crossover dribble, a lethal hesitation move honed on Hampton's playgrounds, sliced through zones like a scalpel, allowing him to explode to the rim with hang time that defied gravity. In his junior year of 1993, Iverson averaged 31.6 points, 10.1 rebounds, and 9.2 assists per game, orchestrating offenses with no-look passes and behind-the-back flair that turned routine plays into spectacles.

Coaches and scouts whispered of his "killer instinct," a refusal to back down that saw him attack bigger opponents without hesitation, absorbing contact and finishing through fouls with a snarl. This fearlessness wasn't recklessness; it was calculated chaos, redefining the guard position from mere facilitator to dominant scorer and playmaker. Peers marveled at his ability to improvise mid-air, contorting layups around shot-blockers or pulling up for jumpers with unteachable rhythm. Local media dubbed him a "phenom," chronicling games where he dropped 38 points against Hopewell, his quickness turning transitions into fast-break clinics. Iverson's style challenged high school norms, inspiring a generation of undersized guards to embrace aggression over caution, proving that heart and ingenuity could eclipse height. In those packed gyms, he wasn't just playing; he was revolutionizing, forging a blueprint for the modern NBA guard from the heart of Virginia's Peninsula District.

In the heart of Hampton's Black communities, Allen Iverson transcended the role of mere athlete, emerging as a living emblem of hope amid the suffocating veil of systemic neglect. To the elders who gathered on stoops, recounting tales of lost promise, Iverson's exploits offered a flicker of possibility—that talent could pierce the barriers of poverty and prejudice. Young kids idolized him, mimicking his crossover on makeshift hoops nailed to telephone poles, seeing in "Bubba Chuck" a blueprint for escape from the cycle of drugs, incarceration, and dead-end jobs that claimed so many. His dual-sport triumphs weren't just personal victories; they were communal anthems, broadcast on local radio and splashed across newspaper headlines, uniting fractured neighborhoods in rare moments of pride. Iverson represented the unpolished diamond from the projects, proof that Hampton's grit could birth greatness, inspiring murals on abandoned walls and whispers of "He's our way out."

Yet, this symbolism carried a crushing weight for a teenager still navigating adolescence. Expectations mounted like storm clouds: coaches demanded flawless performances to attract college scouts, family leaned on him as the beacon to lift them from welfare's grasp, and peers pressured him to stay loyal to the streets while ascending beyond them. Media scrutiny amplified every misstep—the 1993 bowling alley incident, where racial undertones fueled his conviction, turned him into a lightning rod for debates on justice and opportunity. At 17, Iverson bore the invisible yoke of representation: succeed not just for himself, but to validate the dreams of an entire community, or fail and reinforce the narrative of inevitable downfall. This duality forged a complex psyche—fueled by adulation, haunted by the fear of letting down those who saw their reflections in his rise.

As Allen Iverson's star ascended in the early 1990s, his exploits on Bethel's fields and courts ignited a fervor that rippled through Hampton and beyond, drawing college recruiters from Syracuse to Georgetown. Admiration swelled like a tide: community leaders hailed him as a role model, his jerseys became talismans for aspiring youth, and local businesses sponsored banners celebrating his championships. Iverson's raw charisma—flashing cornrows, tattoos emerging as badges of identity—embodied unfiltered Black excellence, inspiring pride in a city starved for positive narratives. Fans packed stadiums, chanting his name, seeing in him the promise of transcendence, a kid from the projects poised to rewrite the script of limitation.

Yet, this burgeoning profile bred tension, fracturing public perception along fault lines of race and class. The infamous 1993 Valentine's Day brawl at a Newport News bowling alley—a chaotic melee sparked by racial slurs—thrust Iverson into controversy. Arrested alongside friends, he was convicted of "maiming by mob," a charge critics decried as archaic and selectively applied to Black teens. Supporters rallied, viewing the trial as a modern lynching, with over 1,000 petitioners demanding justice and Governor Douglas Wilder eventually granting clemency after four months in prison. Detractors, however, painted him as a troublemaker, a volatile talent whose street affiliations threatened to derail his potential. Media outlets amplified the divide: Black press defended his innocence, while mainstream narratives questioned his character, branding him a "thug" archetype. This schism weighed on Iverson, sharpening his distrust of authority and fueling a defiant persona that would define his career—hero to the marginalized, enigma to the establishment.

On the evening of February 14, 1993, Circle Lanes bowling alley in Hampton, Virginia, buzzed with the typical energy of a holiday outing. Located in the Peninsula region, the venue was a popular spot for local high school students, drawing crowds from nearby Bethel and other schools. That Valentine's Day, groups of Black and white teenagers mingled amid the clatter of pins, arcade games, and casual conversations, creating an atmosphere of youthful recreation tinged with underlying social tensions reflective of the area's racial divides.

The incident began when an argument erupted between Iverson's group of friends, who were Black, and a group of white students from Poquoson High School. Witnesses later reported that racial slurs were exchanged, escalating the verbal dispute into a physical melee involving thrown chairs, punches, and chaos that engulfed the alley. Iverson, then 17, was accused by some of striking a white woman, Lynne Luebke, on the head with a chair, causing injuries that required stitches; he and his supporters maintained he was not directly involved in the violence and was attempting to leave. The brawl lasted several minutes, resulting in minor injuries to multiple participants and significant property damage.

Police arrived shortly after, breaking up the fight and detaining those present. Iverson and three Black friends—Samuel Wynn, Michael Simmons, and Melvin Stephens—were arrested that night on charges including maiming by mob, an obscure Virginia statute originally aimed at lynchings but applied here to group assaults. No white participants were charged, a disparity that fueled immediate controversy. Iverson was held in jail pending trial, marking the start of a legal ordeal that would interrupt his senior year and draw national attention to issues of race and justice in the community.

The 1993 bowling alley incident swiftly transcended a mere teenage scuffle, igniting a cultural flashpoint that exposed Hampton's festering racial wounds and reverberated nationally. Rooted in racial dynamics, the brawl erupted amid slurs hurled at Iverson's group, highlighting the Peninsula's segregated undercurrents—Black youths from urban neighborhoods clashing with white teens from suburban Poquoson. The disparity in arrests—four Black teens charged under the archaic "maiming by mob" statute, with no white participants prosecuted—fueled accusations of systemic bias, evoking echoes of Jim Crow-era injustices in a post-civil rights South.

Media coverage amplified the divide. Local outlets like the Daily Press chronicled the trial with sensational headlines, often portraying Iverson as a "troubled" athlete with a checkered past, a narrative critics decried as coded racism that stereotyped young Black men. National attention from Sports Illustrated and ESPN dissected the case, framing it as a microcosm of America's racial fractures, with editorials debating athletic privilege versus unequal justice. Public reaction polarized the community: Black residents rallied in churches and streets, gathering over 1,000 signatures for clemency petitions and viewing Iverson as a scapegoat; white voices, meanwhile, emphasized law and order, decrying special treatment for stars.

This maelstrom reshaped Iverson's narrative—from unadulterated local hero to a contentious symbol of resilience against prejudice. The ordeal branded him with a "thug" label that dogged his career, yet it also galvanized his defiance, transforming personal hardship into a broader commentary on race, opportunity, and redemption in sports.

In the stark confines of Newport News City Farm, a juvenile correctional facility masquerading as a work farm, Allen Iverson's world contracted to cinder-block walls and regimented days that began at dawn. Sentenced to five years but serving only four months after his July 1993 conviction, the 17-year-old phenom traded championship glory for menial labor—picking weeds, cleaning stables—under the watchful eyes of guards who treated him like any other inmate. The emotional weight pressed relentlessly: isolation gnawed at his spirit, nights filled with the echoes of distant sobs and his own suppressed rage. Stripped of freedom, Iverson grappled with betrayal—by a system that seemed rigged against Black youth—and profound loss, missing senior year milestones, family visits limited to tearful glimpses through glass. Letters from his mother, Ann, became lifelines, urging resilience amid his simmering anger at the racial inequities that landed him there.

Personal reflection bloomed in the quiet hours. Iverson confronted his impulsivity, the street code that fueled the brawl, and the fragility of his dreams.

Journaling sporadically, he vowed to channel the pain into fuel, emerging not broken but hardened, his defiance sharpened into a quiet determination. "I ain't gonna let this define me," he later recalled, a mantra born from introspection that fortified his warrior ethos.

Culturally, his incarceration resonated as a stark emblem of America's racial divide, spotlighting how promising Black athletes could be derailed by biased justice. Protests and petitions underscored the narrative: Iverson as victim of a "modern-day lynching," his case amplifying discussions on systemic racism in the courts. Released in December 1993 via Governor Wilder's conditional clemency, he carried the scar as a badge, transforming personal ordeal into a broader symbol of endurance for marginalized communities.

In the wake of Allen Iverson's conviction, Hampton's Black community mobilized with a fervor born of shared injustice, transforming a personal tragedy into a collective crusade for redemption. Churches became rallying points, where pastors and activists like those from the local NAACP chapter organized prayer vigils and protest marches, decrying the charges as racially motivated overreach. Over 1,000 signatures flooded petitions demanding a review, framing Iverson not as a delinquent but as a victim of a system that disproportionately punished Black youth. High-profile figures amplified the call: civil rights leaders drew parallels to historical miscarriages of justice, while supporters flooded Governor L. Douglas Wilder's office with letters, urging clemency for the teen whose talent promised communal uplift.

Legal battles unfolded with relentless determination. Iverson's defense team, led by attorneys like James Ellenson, appealed the verdict, arguing insufficient evidence and bias in the all-white jury's decision. The "maiming by mob" statute, a relic from anti-lynching laws ironically wielded against Black defendants, became a focal point of scrutiny. After four months at City Farm, Wilder granted conditional clemency on December 30, 1993, citing reasonable doubt and Iverson's potential, allowing him to pursue a GED and college basketball. The fight persisted; in 1995, the Virginia Court of Appeals overturned the convictions entirely, vindicating the community's stance.

This unified push reflected a deeper resolve: to salvage a symbol of hope from the jaws of despair. Neighbors fundraised for legal fees, mentors like Boo Williams advocated tirelessly, and even skeptics recognized the stakes—losing Iverson meant extinguishing a light for the next generation. Through activism and advocacy, Hampton's determination secured his second chance, proving that collective will could bend the arc of fate.

Emerging from the gates of City Farm on December 30, 1993, Allen Iverson stepped into a world forever altered, the chill Virginia air carrying both freedom and the ghosts of confinement. At 18, the once-unbridled phenom returned to Hampton not as a defeated youth, but with a profound shift in perspective—a hardened clarity forged in isolation. The ordeal had stripped away illusions: the fragility of fame, the sting of racial injustice, and the peril of unchecked impulses. No longer the carefree "Bubba Chuck" who ruled local courts, Iverson internalized a sobering truth—that survival demanded not just talent, but strategic resolve. He pursued his GED with quiet intensity, enrolling at an alternative school where mentors like Coach Gary Moore emphasized education as armor against recurrence.

This period marked explosive personal growth. Reflection became his silent companion; in conversations with Ann and supporters, he dissected the brawl's chaos, acknowledging how street loyalty had nearly extinguished his dreams. Vulnerability, once buried under bravado, surfaced in rare admissions of fear, fostering empathy for those ensnared in similar cycles. The weight of community advocacy humbled him, transforming gratitude into purpose—he owed his second chance not to luck, but to collective faith, vowing to repay it through excellence.

A new determination ignited like a fuse: basketball became his singular path, abandoning football's allure for Georgetown's offer under Coach John Thompson, a paternal figure who promised structure. Iverson's mindset evolved from defiance to disciplined fire—proving detractors wrong, uplifting Hampton, and redefining success on his terms. This turning point didn't erase scars; it alchemized them into unyielding drive, propelling the phenom toward a destiny that would reshape basketball's cultural landscape.

In the shadowed corridors of redemption, John Thompson Jr. emerged as a towering figure—literally and figuratively—for Allen Iverson. The Georgetown University coach, a 6'10" giant who had transformed the Hoyas into an NCAA powerhouse, boasting national championships in 1984 and Final Four appearances, spotted untapped potential in the beleaguered teen. Thompson, a no-nonsense mentor with a gravelly voice and unyielding principles, had built his legacy on developing Black athletes like Patrick Ewing and Alonzo Mourning, emphasizing character amid talent. In early 1994, as other programs recoiled from Iverson's legal scars—Florida State and Kentucky among those withdrawing offers—Thompson extended a lifeline, personally vouching for him after clemency. "I see myself in you," Thompson reportedly told Iverson, recognizing the fire of a street survivor.

Georgetown represented a singular opportunity, a confluence of cultural, academic, and athletic synergies tailored to Iverson's fractured path. Culturally, it resonated deeply: located in Washington, D.C.'s urban pulse, the Jesuit institution under Thompson fostered a Black excellence ethos, shielding players from exploitation while instilling pride in heritage. Thompson's paternal guidance—strict curfews, mandatory study halls—mirrored the structure Iverson craved, addressing his distrust of authority with tough love rooted in shared experiences of racial adversity.

Academically, the program prioritized graduation, a rarity in big-time college sports, helping Iverson bridge his GED to coursework amid skepticism about his readiness. Athletically, the Big East's bruising competition honed guards like Iverson, allowing his speed and flair to flourish against elite foes, far from the diluted spotlight of lesser conferences. This wasn't just a scholarship; it was salvation, a platform where Iverson could rewrite his narrative, proving that from Hampton's ashes, a phenom could rise unbowed.

As the summer of 1994 waned, Allen Iverson stood on the precipice of departure, his duffel bag packed with the bare essentials—faded jerseys, a worn basketball, and letters from Ann that carried the scent of home. Hampton's streets, once a labyrinth of peril and promise, now felt like a fading echo, their cracked sidewalks etched with memories of triumphs and trials. The community that had rallied for his freedom now gathered in quiet send-offs: barbecues where elders imparted final wisdom, kids clutching autographs as if holding onto a piece of their own dreams. Iverson's eyes, once shadowed by defiance, gleamed with a mix of gratitude and resolve, the weight of expectations now a harness rather than a chain. "This ain't goodbye," he told his siblings, hugging them tight, "it's just the next play."

John Thompson's call had been the catalyst, Georgetown a distant beacon pulling him from the Tidewater's grasp toward the nation's capital. Yet, leaving meant severing ties to the very forces that forged him—the poverty that fueled his hunger, the streets that sharpened his edge, the love that anchored his soul. As Ann watched him board the bus, tears mingling with pride, Iverson felt the emotional surge: fear of the unknown clashing with the fire of reinvention. Hampton had birthed a phenom, but the world beyond awaited, ready to test the limits of his unyielding spirit. With each mile, the chapter of origins closed, propelling him into uncharted territory where culture itself would bend to his will.

Georgetown: The Making of a Rebel Icon

In the sweltering summer of 1994, Allen Iverson stepped off a bus in Washington, D.C., his duffel bag slung over one shoulder like a reluctant anchor. Hampton, Virginia, receded in the rearview—a gritty coastal town where poverty clung to the streets like humidity, where sewage pipes burst into homes and violence erupted in bowling alleys. At 19, Iverson carried the scars of it all: a childhood marked by his mother's addiction, absent father, and the infamous brawl that landed him in jail for four months, only to be pardoned by the governor. Georgetown University loomed ahead, its Gothic spires and manicured lawns a world apart from the cracked sidewalks of his youth. This was no mere relocation; it was an emotional severance, a deliberate shedding of the chaos that had defined him.

The culture shock hit like a full-court press. Georgetown, with its elite pedigree and predominantly white, affluent student body, felt alien to a kid from the projects who braided his hair in cornrows and spoke in the rhythmic cadence of the streets. Classrooms buzzed with debates on philosophy and policy, while Iverson grappled with remedial courses to catch up academically. Yet, amid the disorientation, a sense of rebirth stirred. Coach John Thompson Jr., the towering figure who had recruited him sight unseen, offered not just a scholarship but salvation—a protective shield against the skepticism that trailed Iverson like a shadow. Thompson's program, built on discipline and Black empowerment, promised transformation. For Iverson, it was a chance to rewrite his narrative, to channel the raw energy of Hampton's hardships into something transcendent.

But the weight of his past pressed down relentlessly. Whispers followed him across campus: the felon, the thug, the risk. Every late-night study session, every grueling practice, carried the burden of proving doubters wrong—not just for himself, but for his family back home, scraping by without him. Hampton's ghosts lingered in his dreams, a reminder that escape was fragile, that one misstep could drag him back. Still, in the echoing halls of McDonough Gymnasium, Iverson began to glimpse possibility, his crossover dribble a metaphor for the cultural tightrope he now walked.

Georgetown basketball under John Thompson Jr. wasn't just a program; it was a fortress of defiance, a mythology forged in the fires of racial reckoning and athletic dominance. By the mid-1990s, the Hoyas embodied a national identity as the unyielding bastion of Black excellence in college hoops, a narrative that traced back to Thompson's arrival in 1972. Hired to revive a moribund team at a Jesuit university in the nation's capital, the 6-foot-10 former NBA player transformed Georgetown into a powerhouse, culminating in the 1984

NCAA championship—the first won by a Black head coach. With stars like Patrick Ewing, Alonzo Mourning, and Dikembe Mutombo, Thompson built a legacy of towering centers and ferocious defense, but his true mythology lay in his unapologetic advocacy. He walked off the court in protest against Proposition 42, a rule he saw as discriminatory toward underprivileged Black athletes, and shielded his players from media scrutiny with a towel-draped intensity that became iconic.

This lineage mattered culturally because it represented more than wins; it was a symbol of rebellion against systemic barriers. Georgetown basketball stood as a beacon for young Black men from urban America, proving that street-honed talent could thrive in elite academia without assimilation. For Iverson, stepping into this heritage was profound—a cultural baptism that elevated his personal redemption to a collective statement. Thompson's program didn't just recruit; it reclaimed narratives, turning potential "risks" into icons. In an era when college sports often exploited Black labor while enforcing conformity, Georgetown's ethos of protection and pride offered Iverson a platform to challenge stereotypes. His cornrows and tattoos, once markers of otherness in Hampton, now aligned with the Hoyas' defiant swagger, amplifying a national conversation on identity and authenticity. Entering this storied fold wasn't mere opportunity; it was inheritance, a chance to etch his name into a mythology that redefined what it meant to be a rebel in American sports.

John Thompson Jr. stood as the indomitable architect of Georgetown's mythology, his philosophy rooted in unyielding defense, personal accountability, and fierce advocacy for Black athletes in a system often rigged against them. At 6-foot-10, with a voice that boomed like thunder and a gaze that pierced excuses, Thompson preached a gospel of resilience: offense might falter, but defense—both on the court and in life—demanded constant vigilance. He instilled discipline not through rote drills alone, but by weaving academics into the fabric of success, insisting that degrees were as vital as championships. His mentoring style blended tough love with paternal protection; he shielded players from predatory media, draping towels over cameras during press conferences, while privately pushing them toward self-reliance. Profanity-laced tirades coexisted with life lessons on dignity and perseverance, turning raw talent into fortified character.

For Iverson, Thompson emerged as the ideal guide through his turbulent transition, a towering figure who saw potential where others saw peril. Having recruited Iverson without a campus visit, based solely on reputation and resilience, Thompson became a surrogate father, defending him against critics who branded the young guard a liability. His philosophy aligned perfectly with Iverson's needs: structure to tame the chaos of Hampton, empowerment to embrace his authenticity without apology. Thompson's history of protesting discriminatory policies, like walking off the court over Proposition 42, resonated with Iverson's own battles against injustice. In this crucible, Thompson didn't just coach basketball; he mentored survival, teaching Iverson to navigate elite spaces while honoring his roots. This bond forged Iverson's rebellion into purpose, transforming cultural friction into fuel for greatness.

Georgetown's basketball program under John Thompson Jr. operated like a well-oiled machine, its structure a blend of military precision and academic rigor designed to forge not just athletes, but men equipped for life's battles. Practices were grueling marathons, starting at dawn with defensive drills that emphasized positioning, footwork, and unrelenting pressure—Thompson's hallmark "defend or die" ethos. Offense flowed from this foundation, but sloppiness invited bench time or worse. The daily regimen included weight training, film study, and scrimmages that simulated game intensity, all within a framework that prioritized team cohesion over individual flair. Academic expectations were non-negotiable: players attended mandatory study halls, maintained GPAs, and pursued degrees, with Thompson viewing education as the ultimate equalizer for Black athletes in a skeptical world. Scholarships came with strings—academic probation meant suspension, and Thompson had no qualms about sidelining stars who faltered.

Iverson, fresh from Hampton's unstructured streets, initially chafed against this seriousness. Having missed a year of organized play due to incarceration, he arrived out of shape and unaccustomed to regimented schedules. Yet, adaptation came swiftly on the court; in his first exhibition game against Fort Hood in November 1994, he erupted for 36 points in 23 minutes, showcasing his lightning-quick crossover and scoring instincts within Thompson's system. Academically, he navigated remedial classes and study sessions, bolstered by tutors and Thompson's watchful eye, which shielded him from distractions while demanding accountability. Whispers of his past fueled motivation, turning potential rebellion into resolve. By his freshman season, Iverson started 29 of 30 games, averaging 20.4 points while embracing defensive responsibilities, earning Big East Rookie of the Year honors. The program's discipline honed his raw talent, tempering impulsiveness with strategy, as he learned to channel street-ball creativity into structured plays. This transformation wasn't seamless—taunts from opposing fans tested his composure, prompting Thompson to nearly forfeit a game—but Iverson's growth reflected the program's power: a rebel molded into a disciplined force, ready to redefine college basketball.

In the dim confines of McDonough Gymnasium, Iverson's early practices in October 1994 unfolded like a high-stakes audition, his lithe frame darting amid taller, more seasoned Hoyas under Thompson's watchful glare.

Fresh off a summer of informal runs in the Kenner League—where he had dropped 40 points in his debut game, followed by 33 and 26 in subsequent outings— Iverson brought an electric unpredictability to drills. His crossover dribble, not yet the signature weapon it would become, sliced through defenses with street-ball flair, but Thompson's system demanded precision: defensive slides, help rotations, and relentless conditioning to build stamina for the guard's undersized 6-foot build. Teammates, including veterans like Othella Harrington and Jerome Williams, initially eyed him with a mix of curiosity and skepticism, aware of his controversial past but unprepared for his raw velocity. In scrimmages, Iverson's explosiveness left them reeling—quick bursts to the rim, acrobatic finishes, and an instinctive knack for steals that disrupted plays before they formed.

The immediate impact crystallized in his exhibition debut against Fort Hood on November 8, 1994, before a packed house of 2,432. Inserted two minutes in, Iverson erupted for 24 points in the next eight minutes, 28 by halftime, and 36 overall on efficient shooting, his speed turning the game into a blur. Teammates' reactions shifted from wariness to awe; Harrington later recalled the gym buzzing with murmurs of disbelief, while Williams marveled at how Iverson's quickness elevated everyone's intensity. Recruiting analyst Tom Konchalski, who witnessed his summer exploits, deemed him "the most gifted player I've ever seen," more explosive than NBA stars like Kenny Anderson. Washington Post columnist Thomas Boswell captured the sentiment, calling Iverson "the most exciting unproven teenager I've seen since Alcindor." Even opponents felt the ripple—North Carolina's Dean Smith, after a later matchup, labeled him a "remarkable athlete." Yet, amid the hype, Iverson remained grounded, absorbing Thompson's critiques to refine his game, his explosiveness not just a gift but a tool honed in the forge of Georgetown's demanding practices.

On November 27, 1994, in the cavernous Pyramid arena in Memphis, Tennessee, Allen Iverson made his regular-season debut for Georgetown against the top-ranked, defending national champion Arkansas Razorbacks—a matchup steeped in symbolism, pitting Thompson's defiant Hoyas against Nolan Richardson's high-octane press. Before a crowd of 18,245 and a national television audience tuning into the Black Coaches Association's Martin Luther King Classic, Iverson exploded onto the scene with a performance that, despite its flaws, crackled with raw electricity. Playing 29 minutes, he scored 19 points on 5-of-18 shooting, including three treys, while dishing two assists and snaring a steal. But the numbers belied the spectacle: his blistering speed dismantled Arkansas's vaunted defense in bursts, drawing gasps with crossover dribbles and fearless drives that hinted at a new era of guard play. Eight turnovers spoke to freshman nerves and the Razorbacks' relentless pressure, yet Arkansas coach Nolan Richardson, in postgame remarks, heralded Iverson's uniqueness, underscoring the rookie's potential to redefine the game.

The debut ignited national attention almost instantaneously. Media outlets, from The New York Times to Sports Illustrated, dissected his every move, amplifying the hype that had simmered since his Kenner League exploits and exhibition outbursts. Iverson's street-infused style—cornrows swaying, tattoos peeking from his jersey—clashed vividly with college basketball's polished veneer, generating a cultural buzz that transcended stats. He became an instant symbol of urban authenticity invading elite spaces, a narrative fueled by his Hampton backstory and Thompson's protective aura. Pundits drew comparisons to legends like Kareem Abdul-Jabbar, while Black media celebrated him as a beacon of resilience amid systemic doubts. This wasn't just a game; it was a cultural flashpoint, where Iverson's explosiveness challenged norms, sparking debates on race, redemption, and rebellion in sports. As whispers rippled through barbershops and boardrooms, Iverson's iconography began to crystallize, his debut a harbinger of the seismic waves he would send through the sport.

Within the relentless framework of Georgetown's system, Iverson's offensive decision-making underwent a profound refinement, evolving from impulsive street-ball instincts into a calculated artistry that balanced flair with efficiency. Thompson's philosophy emphasized structured sets—pick-and-rolls, motion offenses, and spacing that demanded patience amid defensive pressure. Early on, Iverson's debut against Arkansas exposed vulnerabilities: eight turnovers from over-dribbling and forced shots, a remnant of unstructured play. But through film sessions and repetitive drills, Thompson and assistants like Mike Jarvis instilled discernment—teaching him to read help defenses, exploit mismatches, and distribute when doubled. By mid-freshman season, his assist numbers stabilized, averaging 4.5 per game, as he learned to use his speed not just for isolation drives but to collapse defenses and kick out to shooters like Harrington. His field-goal percentage climbed from a shaky 39 percent as a freshman to 48 percent in his sophomore year, reflecting better shot selection: fewer contested pull-ups, more drives to the rim where his quickness drew fouls, leading the Big East in free-throw attempts. This sharpening turned potential chaos into controlled dominance, culminating in a 40-point explosion against Syracuse in 1995, where efficient scoring dismantled a ranked foe.

Defensively, the Hoyas' man-to-man scheme amplified Iverson's innate intensity, molding his gambling tendencies into elite disruption. Thompson's drills focused on anticipation—footwork for on-ball pressure, weak-side help, and recovery—transforming Iverson's quick hands from opportunistic swipes into systematic thefts. He led the Big East in steals both seasons, averaging 3.0 as a freshman and 3.4 as a sophomore, earning Defensive Player of the Year honors in 1996. Practices pitted him against bigger guards, building stamina to harass full-court, his low center of gravity allowing him to mirror dribblers and force turnovers that fueled fast breaks. This intensity not only bolstered Georgetown's vaunted defense—holding opponents under 70 points per game—but elevated Iverson's two-way profile, making him a national force. The system's rigor forged a rebel into a refined predator, his growth a testament to Thompson's blueprint.

Under Thompson's exacting guidance, Iverson's evolution into a fearsome two-way player marked a pivotal chapter in his Georgetown tenure, blending his innate gifts with disciplined execution to terrorize opponents on both ends. Initially, his freshman year revealed flashes of brilliance tempered by inexperience; averaging 20.4 points per game on 39 percent shooting, Iverson's offensive arsenal relied heavily on speed and improvisation, often leading to turnovers in high-pressure scenarios. Thompson's system, however, imposed structure—drills emphasizing ball movement and decision-making under duress gradually refined his choices. By sophomore season, his scoring surged to 25.0 points per game at a crisp 48 percent efficiency, as he mastered pick-and-roll reads and pull-up jumpers, drawing fouls at an elite clip while boosting assists to 4.7 per contest. This offensive maturation didn't dilute his flair; instead, it amplified it, turning chaotic drives into surgical strikes that dismantled defenses.

Defensively, Thompson unlocked Iverson's predatory instincts, channeling his quickness into a suffocating force. Leading the Big East in steals as a freshman with 3.0 per game, he disrupted passing lanes with anticipatory gambles, but Thompson's coaching curbed recklessness, teaching help principles and on-ball tenacity. By 1996, Iverson averaged 3.4 steals, earning Big East Defensive Player of the Year honors while anchoring a Hoyas unit that ranked among the nation's stingiest. His low stance and lateral agility allowed him to harass taller guards, forcing turnovers that ignited fast breaks—epitomizing the two-way guard prototype. Thompson's paternal mentorship, blending fiery rebukes with strategic wisdom, fostered this growth, instilling resilience against taunts and expectations. Iverson's rebounding ticked up modestly to 3.8 per game as a sophomore, but his overall impact transcended numbers: a 6-foot guard who played like a giant, blending offense and defense into unrelenting dominance. This transformation solidified his All-American status, proving Thompson's blueprint could forge street legend into collegiate terror.

As Iverson's on-court exploits intensified, he catapulted into the national spotlight, transforming from a controversial recruit into college basketball's most compelling narrative. By December 1994, after torching Arkansas in his debut and following it with a 40-point dismantling of Providence—where his crossover left defenders grasping at air—media outlets swarmed. Sports Illustrated profiled him as "The Answer," a moniker that stuck, while The Washington Post chronicled his every step, blending awe at his agility with scrutiny of his background. His freshman averages of 20.4 points, 4.5 assists, and 3.0 steals earned Big East Rookie of the Year honors, but the story transcended stats: Iverson's presence ignited a firestorm of coverage, with networks like ESPN replaying his highlights endlessly, positioning him as the heir to Georgetown's legacy of dominance. Rivalries amplified the hype—clashes with UConn's Ray Allen or St. John's Felipe Lopez drew record crowds, framing Iverson as the undersized underdog rewriting guard play.

Culturally, discussions swirled around his unapologetic persona, a lightning rod for debates on race, class, and authenticity in sports. His cornrows, baggy shorts, and tattoos—emblems of Hampton's streets—clashed with the sport's buttoned-up image, sparking conversations in Black media about empowerment and in mainstream outlets about "thug culture." Pundits questioned whether his style signaled rebellion or progress, while urban youth saw a mirror: a player who fused hip-hop swagger with elite skill, challenging the assimilation demanded of Black athletes. Thompson's protective stance fueled the discourse, portraying Iverson as a symbol of resilience amid systemic skepticism. By his sophomore year, with All-American nods and a 25-point average, Iverson wasn't just a star; he embodied a cultural shift, his narrative weaving personal redemption into broader dialogues on identity in American athletics.

Amid the acclaim, Iverson's tenure at Georgetown simmered with an undercurrent of friction, a clash between his street-informed creativity and the program's ironclad disciplined identity. Rooted in Hampton's asphalt courts, Iverson's game pulsed with improvisation—a crossover born of survival instincts, drives that defied structure, and a flair that prioritized spectacle over system.

Thompson's Georgetown, however, demanded conformity to a blueprint of defensive rigidity and offensive precision, where individualism bowed to collective execution. This tension manifested early: in practices, Iverson's freelance dribbling often disrupted sets, drawing Thompson's thunderous rebukes, his voice echoing like judgment in the gym. "Play within the team," Thompson would bark, insisting that street-ball wizardry, while electric, invited chaos in high-stakes games. Iverson's tattoos and cornrows, symbols of unfiltered authenticity, amplified the divide, clashing with the Hoyas' polished Jesuit ethos and drawing campus stares that underscored his outsider status.

Yet, this friction wasn't merely destructive; it fueled a dynamic evolution, a cultural negotiation that reshaped both player and program. Iverson pushed boundaries, injecting hip-hop rhythm into Georgetown's stoic framework—his no-look passes and ankle-breaking moves challenging the status quo while forcing teammates to adapt to his pace. Thompson, ever the protector, navigated this by blending stern guidance with subtle allowances, recognizing that stifling Iverson's essence would dim his brilliance. Off-court, the strain extended to academics and visibility: mandatory study halls chafed against his free-spirited upbringing, while national media scrutiny painted him as a "thug" archetype, heightening the pressure to conform. Defining moments, like a heated exchange during a 1995 loss to Villanova where Iverson's turnovers sparked a benching, highlighted the rub—his creativity sparking brilliance one play, recklessness the next. Through it all, the disciplined identity tempered Iverson's edges without erasing them, forging a hybrid style that symbolized broader cultural tensions in Black athletics: the pull between assimilation and rebellion, structure and soul. This alchemy not only sustained Georgetown's relevance but positioned Iverson as a harbinger of change, his friction a catalyst for the sport's shifting paradigms.

On the manicured quads of Georgetown University, Allen Iverson emerged as an enigmatic campus figure, a 6-foot whirlwind whose presence disrupted the elite calm of the Jesuit institution. Amid students in khakis and polos, Iverson moved with a street-born swagger—cornrows cascading, tattoos narrating tales of survival—that turned heads and sparked whispers. He wasn't just a basketball player; he became a living emblem, mobbed in dining halls for autographs, his dorm a hub for admirers drawn to his unfiltered aura. Yet, solitude shadowed his stardom; protective barriers erected by Thompson limited interactions, fostering an air of mystery that amplified his allure. Iverson's late-night walks across campus, headphones blaring hip-hop, symbolized a bridge between worlds: the projects of Hampton infiltrating ivory towers.

Within Black culture, Iverson crystallized as a symbol of defiant resilience, a testament to Thompson's ethos of unapologetic excellence. His style—baggy jerseys echoing urban fashion, crossover dribbles infused with playground rhythm—resonated as a manifesto against assimilation, echoing the Hoyas' legacy of Black empowerment. Media dubbed him "The Answer," but for Black youth, he was validation: a kid from the hood thriving without code-switching, his cornrows a crown challenging stereotypes. In barbershops and community centers, his highlights sparked pride, positioning him alongside cultural icons like Tupac Shakur—raw, rebellious, and real. Youth culture, spanning inner-city courts to suburban rec leagues, adopted his ethos; white kids braided their hair in mimicry, while Black teens saw possibility in his journey from incarceration to icon. This symbolism extended beyond campus, fueling national dialogues on identity, where Iverson's authenticity confronted the sport's sanitized image. His emergence marked a cultural pivot, blending hip-hop's edge with basketball's grace, making him a beacon for a generation navigating race and rebellion.

Amid the cultural whirlwind enveloping him, Iverson confronted Georgetown's formidable academic demands, a crucible that tested his resolve as much as any on-court rivalry. As a freshman from a high school disrupted by incarceration, he entered under NCAA scrutiny, having completed remedial summer coursework to secure eligibility—a half-credit shy of his diploma, he earned the necessary grades and SAT scores to meet the 2.0 GPA threshold in core subjects. Enrolled in the College of Arts and Sciences with a focus on fine arts, Iverson navigated a curriculum far removed from Hampton's streets: classes in rhetoric, history, and philosophy demanded analytical rigor, while mandatory study halls enforced by Thompson ensured compliance. Tutors shadowed him, dissecting assignments in late-night sessions at McDonough Arena, where basketball film reviews often bled into academic reviews. The Jesuit institution's ethos of intellectual pursuit clashed with his instinctive world, requiring him to master time management amid a schedule packed with practices, travel, and games.

This balancing act between success and responsibility weighed heavily, a high-wire performance where one slip could unravel everything. Iverson's rising stardom amplified the stakes: campus celebrity status brought distractions—autograph seekers, media hounds—yet Thompson's program imposed structure, fining tardiness and suspending for academic lapses. He sent earnings from odd jobs and stipends home to support his mother and siblings, adding emotional ballast to his load. Success on the court, like his 40-point outbursts, fueled motivation, but responsibility loomed larger: proving skeptics wrong by graduating, embodying Thompson's mantra that education outlasted athletics. Tensions flared in moments of fatigue, when road trips blurred into term papers, but Iverson adapted, his GPA stabilizing as he internalized the discipline. This equilibrium forged not just a player, but a man aware that true iconography demanded holistic triumph, his academic grind a silent rebellion against narratives of failure.

Iverson's Georgetown legacy crystallized through a series of electrifying games and heated Big East rivalries that showcased his scoring prowess, defensive tenacity, and unyielding will. His debut against top-ranked Arkansas on November 27, 1994, set the tone: amid a 97-79 loss, the freshman dropped 21 points with audacious drives that stunned the defending champions, announcing his arrival as a national disruptor. Rivalries ignited his fire, particularly against UConn's Ray Allen, whose matchups became legendary. In their February 19, 1996, regular-season clash, Iverson tallied 23 points and 10 assists in a 77-65 Hoyas victory, outdueling Allen in a battle of future NBA stars. But the 1996 Big East Tournament final etched enduring drama: Georgetown fell 75-74 to UConn on Ray Allen's buzzer-beater, with Iverson's 23 points marred by foul trouble and a missed game-winner, highlighting the razor-thin margins of elite competition.

High-scoring outbursts built his mythos. Against Arizona on December 9, 1995, he erupted for a career-high 40 points in a 91-81 win, his crossover dismantling defenders in a display of offensive brilliance. Rival Villanova felt his wrath on January 10, 1996, with 37 points in an 86-69 rout, while St. John's succumbed to his 39-point barrage on February 24, 1996, underscoring his dominance over Big East foes like Syracuse (37 points in a 1995 loss) and Miami (38 points in 1996). Postseason runs amplified his stature: in the 1995 NCAA Tournament, Iverson averaged 23 points across three games, pushing Georgetown to the Sweet 16 before falling to North Carolina. The 1996 tourney saw him average nearly 28 points, including 31 against Mississippi Valley State and Texas Tech, guiding the Hoyas to the Elite Eight in a heartbreaking 83-73 loss to UMass. These performances not only earned him All-American honors but cemented Iverson as Georgetown's rebel leader, his intensity forging a legacy of defiance and excellence amid the conference's cutthroat battles.

Iverson's postseason battles at Georgetown served as crucibles, forging his raw talent into seasoned leadership and sharpening his decision-making under the glare of national stakes. In the 1995 NCAA Tournament, as a freshman thrust into the spotlight, he averaged 23 points over three games, blending explosive scoring with defensive disruptions that propelled the Hoyas to the Sweet 16. Against Weber State, his 21 points and five steals showcased instinctive flair, but the loss to North Carolina—where foul trouble limited him to 24 points—exposed vulnerabilities in composure, turnovers creeping in amid Tar Heel pressure. These high-wire moments demanded adaptation; Thompson's sideline intensity pushed Iverson to temper impulsiveness, fostering a maturation where individual brilliance served the team.

By 1996, the evolution was evident in the Big East Tournament, where Iverson's leadership galvanized Georgetown to the final against UConn. Scoring 23 points despite foul issues, he orchestrated comebacks with precise passes and steals, though Ray Allen's buzzer-beater sealed a 75-74 defeat—a gut-wrenching lesson in clutch execution. The NCAA run amplified this growth: averaging nearly 28 points across four games, including 31 against Mississippi Valley State and Texas Tech, Iverson's decisions reflected poise—fewer forced shots, more facilitation amid double-teams, elevating teammates like Victor Page. The Elite Eight clash with UMass, an 86-62 loss, tested his resolve; down big, Iverson poured in 23 points, refusing surrender, his on-court commands rallying a faltering squad. These battles shaped him beyond stats, instilling a leader's gravitas: the rebel who learned to harness chaos, balancing street creativity with strategic restraint, emerging as Georgetown's emotional core ready for greater horizons.

As Iverson's sophomore season wound down in the spring of 1996, the weight of his journey pressed upon him like an unrelenting full-court defense. Two years at Georgetown had sculpted the raw talent from Hampton's streets into a polished force: All-American honors, Big East Defensive Player of the Year, and averages of 25 points, 4.7 assists, and 3.4 steals that propelled the Hoyas to the Elite Eight. Yet, beneath the accolades simmered personal turmoil—his mother's ongoing struggles with addiction, his younger sister's chronic seizures demanding medical care, and the family's financial precarity back home. Thompson, the steadfast mentor who had shielded him from doubt, now counseled deliberation, emphasizing education's enduring value while acknowledging the NBA's siren call. Iverson's emergence as a cultural icon amplified the stakes; he symbolized

Black resilience, his cornrows and crossover a defiant bridge between urban authenticity and elite achievement, drawing scouts and scrutiny alike.

The decision crystallized amid hushed family discussions and Thompson's paternal guidance: declare for the 1996 NBA Draft, becoming the first under Thompson to leave early. This wasn't mere ambition; it carried emotional freight—a chance to uplift his loved ones, to transcend the ghosts of incarceration and poverty. Culturally, it marked a pivot, challenging college basketball's norms and foreshadowing hip-hop's infusion into the pros. As draft projections pegged him as a top pick, anticipation built like a gathering storm: the rebel icon, forged in Georgetown's fire, stood on the threshold of reinvention, his next crossover poised to redefine the league.

The Draft and The Arrival

In the spring of 1996, Allen Iverson stood at the precipice of a life-altering choice, the air thick with the residue of his improbable journey. At Georgetown University, under the watchful eye of coach John Thompson—a towering figure who had become both mentor and shield—Iverson had reinvented himself. From the shadowed streets of Hampton, Virginia, where a high school brawl had landed him in jail and nearly derailed his future, to the polished courts of the Big East, he had channeled raw fury into basketball brilliance. Averaging 25 points per game in his sophomore season, earning Defensive Player of the Year honors, and leading the Hoyas to the Sweet Sixteen, Iverson had proven his mettle. Yet, the pull of the NBA draft loomed like a siren call, whispering promises of financial security for his family and a platform to transcend the game.

The decision crystallized after Georgetown's tournament exit, a loss that stung but illuminated the path forward. Iverson, ever the stoic warrior, announced his departure on May 2, his voice steady amid the flashing cameras, but the tears in his mother Ann's eyes betrayed the emotional torrent beneath. This was no mere career move; it carried the weight of redemption, of lifting his loved ones from poverty's grip—houses without water or electricity still fresh in memory. Culturally, Iverson's leap symbolized a bridge between street authenticity and mainstream success, a Black athlete from the margins daring to infuse the league with hip-hop swagger and unapologetic grit. Critics murmured about his size, his shot selection, his tattoos hinting at a rebellious edge, but supporters saw destiny: a kid who had survived systemic traps now poised to redefine basketball's narrative.

Stepping into the unknown felt predestined, a culmination of resilience forged in adversity. Iverson's transition wasn't just personal; it echoed the aspirations of a generation, blending athletic prowess with cultural defiance. As draft projections pegged him as a top pick, the anticipation built—a young icon ready to claim his throne.

Scouting reports painted Allen Iverson as a tantalizing enigma, a blend of unparalleled gifts and glaring risks that fueled endless projections. Analysts marveled at his blistering speed—often clocked as the quickest in college basketball—allowing him to blow past defenders with a crossover dribble that left opponents grasping at air. His court vision shone in transition, dishing assists with flair, but weaknesses loomed large: a shoot-first mentality that prioritized pull-up jumpers over team play, leading to erratic decisions and turnovers. Early mocks consistently slotted him at No. 1, ahead of talents like Marcus Camby and Shareef Abdur-Rahim, with projections hinging on his ability to adapt that frenetic style to the pro game's structure. Yet, his height became a flashpoint; officially 6 feet, skeptics whispered he measured closer to 5'10", questioning if such a diminutive frame could endure the NBA's physicality against towering guards.

Media debates swirled with cultural undercurrents, dissecting Iverson's perceived attitude as much as his skills. Outlets like Sports Illustrated and ESPN highlighted his swagger and baggy streetwear as symbols of street authenticity, sparking conversations about hip-hop's infiltration into a league still clinging to polished professionalism. Critics fretted over his "thug" image, rooted in the

Virginia brawl that had scarred his reputation, fearing immaturity might derail his potential. Supporters countered that his defiance represented empowerment for Black youth from urban America, a raw edge that could revitalize the sport. Speed was universally lauded as his superpower, but style critiques painted him as selfish, a solo artist in a symphony. As June approached, these narratives amplified the stakes, positioning Iverson not just as a prospect, but a cultural litmus test for the NBA's evolving identity.

As Allen Iverson's name ascended draft boards in the lead-up to June 1996, cultural conversations about his entry into the NBA deepened, transforming him from a college standout into a lightning rod for debates on image, identity, and broader societal representation. At the core was his unapologetic presentation: tattoos sprawling across his skin like personal hieroglyphs, narrating tales of hardship from Hampton's rough edges, which some viewed as defiant badges of authenticity while others decried them as signals of unruliness threatening the league's upscale image. Media forums buzzed with dissections of his style—baggy clothes echoing hip-hop's oversized silhouette—questioning if this aesthetic would dilute the NBA's appeal to corporate sponsors or inject vital energy into a sport seeking relevance among urban youth.

Identity debates cut even sharper, positioning Iverson as a vessel for Black America's multifaceted narrative. To supporters in Black media and community circles, he represented unfiltered resilience, a young man who had navigated poverty, incarceration, and redemption without shedding his roots, embodying the hip-hop ethos of survival and swagger that resonated with a generation raised on Public Enemy and Tupac. Detractors, often from more conservative sports commentary, worried his perceived "attitude"—a quiet intensity mistaken for arrogance—might reinforce stereotypes, labeling him a potential liability in a league still healing from perceptions of thuggery. What did he truly represent: a cultural bridge fostering inclusivity, or a risk to the polished professionalism that had elevated stars like Magic Johnson? As these dialogues unfolded in columns and talk shows, Iverson's arrival loomed as a referendum on the NBA's willingness to embrace diversity, his image challenging the status quo and hinting at a league on the verge of cultural reinvention.

On June 26, 1996, the Continental Airlines Arena in East Rutherford, New Jersey, pulsed with electric anticipation, a cauldron of spotlights and murmurs as the NBA Draft unfolded before a packed house and millions watching on television. Rows of suited prospects sat rigidly at tables flanked by agents and loved ones, the air thick with tension—whispers of trades, last-minute scouting whispers, and the weight of careers hanging on Commissioner David Stern's every word. Cameras swarmed like predators, capturing every fidget, every hopeful glance, their flashes etching the night into history. For Allen Iverson, positioned at a table with his mother Ann, family members, and close friends, the moment distilled years of strife into a single, breathless pivot. His mindset was a storm of resolve and reflection: the kid from Hampton who had dodged prison bars just three years earlier now eyed the stage with quiet intensity, his short-cropped hair and oversized suit masking the explosive force within. He knew the projections pegged him first, yet doubt lingered—his size, his past, the cultural scrutiny—all amplifying the stakes.

As Stern approached the podium, the arena hushed, hearts pounding in unison. "With the first pick in the 1996 NBA Draft, the Philadelphia 76ers select Allen Iverson from Georgetown University." The crowd erupted in a mix of cheers and gasps, symbolizing the league's gamble on audacity over convention. Iverson rose, embracing his tearful mother and family in a whirlwind of hugs, his face a mask of composed emotion amid the chaos. Backstage glimpses showed him donning the Sixers cap, the gold bracelet on his wrist glinting under the lights, as interviewers probed his readiness. In that instant, Iverson's mindset crystallized—not as a conqueror, but a contributor, eager to blend his speed into a team hungry for revival, the tension dissolving into destiny's embrace.

As Commissioner David Stern's voice boomed through the arena—"With the first pick in the 1996 NBA Draft, the Philadelphia 76ers select Allen Iverson from Georgetown University"—a collective gasp rippled across the crowd, mingling shock with electric jubilation. Iverson, the undersized enigma who had dominated projections yet stirred endless debate, now stood as the top choice, a decision that stunned purists favoring taller, more conventional talents like the seven-foot Marcus Camby. The selection wasn't just a gamble; it was a seismic shift, injecting raw audacity into a league accustomed to measured risks. Iverson rose slowly from his table, his face a canvas of restrained emotion—eyes wide with the weight of validation—as family members enveloped him in a frenzy of embraces. His mother Ann, tears streaming, clutched him tightly, her presence a poignant reminder of the poverty-stricken roots this moment uprooted. Cheers erupted from sections of the arena, while skeptics murmured about his size and style, but the celebration swelled, cameras capturing the gold chain glinting against his suit as he adjusted the Sixers cap atop his head.

Historically, this pick carried profound significance for a beleaguered Philadelphia franchise mired in mediocrity. The 76ers had stumbled to an 18-64 record the prior season, their last playoff appearance a distant memory from 1991, starved for a savior to revive the storied legacy of Wilt Chamberlain and Julius Erving. Selecting Iverson signaled a bold rebuild, prioritizing speed and scoring over height, in a city whose blue-collar ethos craved underdogs with unyielding grit. For Black Philadelphia, it symbolized more: a local-adjacent hero from Virginia's margins, embodying resilience amid urban struggles, poised to infuse the team with cultural authenticity. As confetti fell and handshakes ensued, the shock gave way to destiny's roar, marking Iverson's arrival as a cultural inflection point for the NBA's evolving narrative.

In the wake of Allen Iverson's selection, the Philadelphia 76ers emerged as a franchise teetering on the edge of irrelevance, desperately clawing for renewal amid years of stagnation. By 1996, the team had devolved into a shadow of its former glory, posting a dismal 18-64 record the previous season—their worst since the early 1970s—and missing the playoffs for five straight years. The storied echoes of Wilt Chamberlain's dominance and Julius Erving's aerial artistry had faded, replaced by a revolving door of coaches, underwhelming drafts, and fan apathy in a city that demanded passion. Ownership, under Harold Katz until a recent sale to Comcast Spectacor, recognized the urgent need for a cornerstone—a transcendent talent capable of igniting ticket sales, media buzz, and on-court revival. The Sixers' rebuild was in its infancy, with assets like Jerry Stackhouse from the prior draft offering promise but no anchor. Desperation fueled bold moves: trading for veterans like Derrick Coleman had flopped, leaving a roster starved for leadership and excitement.

Iverson, despite his unconventional profile, embodied the perfect antidote to this malaise. His selection wasn't mere lottery luck; it was a calculated embrace of dynamism over safety. General Manager Brad Greenberg and coach Johnny Davis saw in him a scoring savant whose Georgetown pedigree—leading the Hoyas to elite status—promised immediate impact. At a time when the NBA favored size, Iverson's selection bucked trends, prioritizing his elite speed, handles, and defensive tenacity to disrupt the Eastern Conference's plodding pace. For Philadelphia, a gritty, working-class town with a history of embracing underdogs, Iverson's narrative resonated: a survivor of adversity mirroring the city's own resilience amid economic decline. His arrival signaled hope, a potential franchise face to fill the void left by Charles Barkley's departure years earlier, injecting cultural relevance into a team on life support. As summer loomed, the Sixers' front office buzzed with optimism, viewing Iverson not as a risk, but as the spark to rebuild an empire.

In the electrifying aftermath of his name being called, Allen Iverson's emotional reaction unfolded like a dam breaking, a rare glimpse into the vulnerability beneath his armored exterior. As he stood, his face tightened with a mix of disbelief and quiet triumph, eyes glistening under the arena lights while he enveloped his mother, Ann, in a fierce embrace—her sobs echoing the hardships they had endured together in Hampton's unforgiving streets. Family members piled on, a chaotic circle of joy and tears, as Iverson adjusted the Sixers cap with trembling hands, his gold chain swinging like a pendulum marking time from past to present. Later reflections revealed the depth: the moment overwhelmed him, a surge of gratitude for escaping poverty's clutches—nights without electricity, his mother's sacrifices—now validated by the league's highest honor. It wasn't just relief; it was redemption, a personal vindication after the 1993 brawl that branded him a felon at 17, only for clemency and Georgetown to reroute his fate.

Culturally, this pinnacle resonated as a watershed, amplifying Iverson's role as a beacon for Black America in the 1990s. Being the first overall pick—a diminutive guard with tattoos and unpolished edges—challenged the NBA's sanitized image, symbolizing the mainstreaming of hip-hop authenticity amid debates over "thug" stereotypes. For urban youth, it meant possibility: a survivor from the margins claiming the throne, his past not a barrier but fuel for defiance. In Philadelphia's resilient spirit, Iverson's ascent mirrored the city's own underdog narrative, fostering a bond that would define his legacy. As confetti settled, the moment crystallized his journey—from incarceration's shadow to stardom's glare—igniting a cultural dialogue on identity that echoed far beyond the draft stage.

As the echoes of Commissioner David Stern's announcement faded, national media outlets erupted in a chorus of analysis, blending awe with apprehension over Allen Iverson's ascension to the first overall pick. Sports Illustrated's draft coverage hailed him as a "scintillating talent," emphasizing his Georgetown exploits where he averaged 25 points and dazzled with speed, yet tempered praise with warnings about his 6-foot frame in a league dominated by taller guards. ESPN analysts, in live post-draft breakdowns, debated the gamble: Dick Vitale lauded Iverson's "heart of a lion" and unteachable quickness, predicting he could revitalize the moribund Sixers, while others like Peter Vecsey questioned if his shoot-first style and controversial past would translate amid the NBA's grueling physicality. Newspapers across the country mirrored this duality; The New York Times noted the selection as a bold statement on prioritizing skill over size, but editorials fretted over his "baggage" from the Virginia incident, sparking discussions on redemption in professional sports.

Analysts across scouting circles echoed this divide, with figures from the NBA's own draft room acknowledging the boldness—passing on safer bets like Ray Allen or Kobe Bryant for Iverson's intangibles. Fan responses mirrored the media frenzy; in Philadelphia, sports radio lines lit up with ecstatic callers envisioning a revival, fans packing bars to toast the arrival of a gritty savior whose journey from Hampton's hardships aligned with the city's underdog soul. Nationally, basketball message boards and fan polls buzzed with optimism from urban audiences who saw Iverson as their voice, contrasted by suburban skeptics fretting over his past legal entanglements diluting the game's image. This whirlwind of commentary not only amplified the anticipation but positioned Iverson's entry as a litmus test for the NBA's future, where talent intertwined with cultural narratives in ways that promised to redefine the sport.

With the draft night's confetti settled into memory, Allen Iverson jetted to Philadelphia, stepping into a city and organization humming with cautious optimism. His first interactions unfolded at the CoreStates Spectrum, where a press conference introduced him to a throng of reporters and executives eager to anoint their new cornerstone. Team president Pat Croce, a charismatic former physical therapist with a flair for motivation, greeted Iverson with infectious energy, slapping his back and proclaiming the guard's arrival as the dawn of a new era for the floundering franchise. General manager Brad Greenberg, who had championed Iverson atop the draft board despite internal debates over safer picks, shook his hand firmly, outlining visions of a high-octane offense built around his speed and scoring. Head coach Johnny Davis, freshly installed after a turbulent coaching carousel, pulled Iverson aside for a brief huddle, emphasizing discipline and team integration while praising his Georgetown film as a blueprint for revival.

The organizational culture Iverson encountered was one of raw ambition amid reconstruction— a front office desperate to shed years of losing, blending veteran holdovers like Clarence Weatherspoon with young talents like Jerry Stackhouse, all under the shadow of fan impatience. Philadelphia's ethos amplified this: a blue-collar metropolis where sports loyalty bordered on religion, expectations soared for underdogs who bled effort, yet pressure crushed those who faltered. Iverson, with his quiet confidence and street-honed edge, navigated these early exchanges thoughtfully, expressing gratitude for the opportunity while absorbing the city's unyielding gaze. These moments seeded a bond, hinting at the cultural fusion ahead, as Iverson's authenticity began to mesh with Philly's gritty soul.

Philadelphia, in the summer of 1996, enveloped Allen Iverson like a relentless embrace—equal parts welcoming and unforgiving, a city forged in the fires of American grit and unyielding passion. Known as the City of Brotherly Love, its sports scene pulsed with an intensity that bordered on obsession, fans packing arenas with blue-collar fervor, their cheers a thunderous demand for effort over excuses. The history loomed large: cradle of independence, home to revolutionary spirits, but also a metropolis scarred by economic decline, racial tensions, and industrial decay in the post-manufacturing era. Basketball held sacred ground here, from the Big Five college rivalries to the 76ers' golden epochs with legends like Wilt Chamberlain, who shattered records in the 1960s, and Julius Erving, whose soaring dunks defined the 1980s championship run. Yet, by Iverson's arrival, the franchise's glory had dimmed, fans starved for a hero amid years of losing seasons, their expectations soaring sky-high for any spark of revival.

This environment proved both perfect and perilous for Iverson. His own story of resilience—rising from Hampton's poverty and legal pitfalls—mirrored Philly's underdog ethos, a shared narrative of defiance against odds that fostered an instant bond. The city's fans craved authenticity, rewarding players who poured sweat and soul, much like Iverson's fearless drives to the basket. Yet, the challenges were stark: the scrutiny was merciless, boos raining down on underperformers, and the pressure to single-handedly resurrect a team could crush lesser wills. Iverson's edgy persona, with its street-smart flair, aligned with Philly's raw energy, promising a symbiotic explosion of excitement. But in a town where loyalty was earned through grit, not gifted, he faced the daunting task of proving his mettle amid high stakes, making Philadelphia the ultimate proving ground for his ascent.

As summer gave way to autumn in 1996, Allen Iverson descended upon the Philadelphia 76ers' training camp at La Salle University, a compact whirlwind of energy amid a roster desperate for direction. The camp, kicking off in early October, marked his first immersion in professional rigors—grueling two-a-days, film sessions, and scrimmages designed to forge cohesion from chaos. Iverson arrived with his trademark intensity, dazzling coaches with blistering speed and instinctive scoring that evoked comparisons to undersized greats like Isiah Thomas. Yet, adjustments loomed large; accustomed to Georgetown's structured system under John Thompson, he grappled with the NBA's faster pace, deeper defenses, and emphasis on efficiency. Early practices revealed flashes of brilliance—crossover dribbles slicing through veterans, pull-up jumpers raining in—but also raw edges: erratic shot selection, turnovers from forcing plays, and a need to balance individualism with team flow.

Organizational reactions mixed awe with caution. Head coach Johnny Davis, in his first full season, praised Iverson's raw talent and scoring prowess, noting his potential to anchor the rebuild, but flagged immaturity in minor latenesses—12 or 13 instances over the year, often just minutes tardy. Executives like Brad Greenberg viewed him as a cornerstone, yet worried his style clashed with Jerry Stackhouse's similar ball-dominant approach, sparking internal debates on lineup harmony. Teammates, including veterans like Clarence Weatherspoon, appreciated Iverson's work ethic on the court—playing hard every drill, never shying from contact—but whispered about his casual approach to punctuality, a holdover from college freedoms. As camp progressed, Iverson adapted incrementally, absorbing feedback on defensive positioning and playmaking, his quiet determination earning respect amid the sweat-soaked sessions. The Sixers' brass saw promise in his grit, a spark for a franchise in flux, even as his unpolished edges hinted at the challenges ahead.

As training camp intensified, reactions within the Philadelphia 76ers organization to Allen Iverson's arrival rippled through every level, a mix of exhilaration and measured concern that highlighted his raw potential against the backdrop of a rebuilding team. Head coach Johnny Davis, tasked with molding the rookie into a true point guard, marveled at Iverson's fearlessness—a daring willingness to attack the rim against bigger bodies, driving through contact with an abandon that left defenders reeling. "He's a young stallion," Davis remarked, emphasizing the need to harness that spirit without breaking it, as Iverson's Georgetown scoring instincts clashed with the NBA's demand for playmaking. Yet, Davis also addressed punctuality issues early, benching Iverson briefly for tardiness to a game, underscoring a front office push for professionalism amid the hype.

Veterans like Clarence Weatherspoon and Derrick Coleman observed Iverson's blazing speed with awe, his quickness turning scrimmages into showcases where he blew past defenders, dishing or finishing with equal flair. Weatherspoon, the team's steady forward, noted Iverson's presence as electric, a magnetic force that energized practices but demanded adjustment from ball-dominant teammates like Jerry Stackhouse. Stackhouse, entering his second year, clashed with Iverson over touches, leading to a heated altercation at a 1997 shootaround, later reflecting that the lack of seasoned vets hindered their cohesion. Front office executives, including general manager Brad Greenberg, celebrated Iverson's intangibles—his unyielding presence commanding respect despite his size—as the key to revival, though whispers of immaturity tempered the optimism. Veteran Tom Chambers even offered to drive Iverson to practices to curb lateness, only for the rookie to decline humorously, insisting he alone could fix it. These early dynamics painted Iverson as a transformative spark, his fearlessness and speed injecting life into a stagnant squad, even as his presence tested the organization's patience.

As preseason games loomed in October 1996, Allen Iverson plunged into the NBA's unforgiving ecosystem, a far cry from Georgetown's collegiate cocoon. Adaptation demanded a recalibration of habits forged in survival mode, where discipline emerged as the first hurdle. Coach Johnny Davis, sensing Iverson's casual approach to time—rooted in a life of unstructured chaos—imposed structure, fining him for latenesses that dotted early sessions. Iverson, ever resilient, absorbed the lessons, arriving earlier as the weeks wore on, his quiet determination transforming minor infractions into stepping stones. The professional grind tested his endurance: an 82-game slate loomed like an endless marathon, with back-to-backs, cross-country flights, and relentless physicality that battered his 165-pound frame. Bruises from drives accumulated, teaching him the art of pacing amid the league's nightly wars.

Film study became a revelation, hours spent in dimly lit rooms dissecting opponents' tendencies—learning to read pick-and-rolls, anticipate double-teams, and refine his shot selection beyond instinctual flair. Veterans like Derrick Coleman guided him through tapes, pointing out nuances Iverson's speed alone couldn't conquer, fostering a deeper basketball IQ. Press responsibilities amplified the pressure; as the franchise's face, he faced daily scrums, cameras probing his past and potential, his terse responses evolving into measured candor under media training. The scrutiny mirrored his cultural spotlight, where every misstep fueled narratives of immaturity. Yet, Iverson embraced the grind's rhythm, his work ethic shining in extra gym time, blending street-honed grit with pro polish. This period marked his metamorphosis, from raw talent to emerging professional, the NBA's demands forging a sharper edge amid Philadelphia's expectant gaze.

When preseason murmurs turned to roars in late 1996, Philadelphia's reaction to Allen Iverson's arrival swirled with a potent cocktail of anticipation and hype, a city starved for basketball salvation after years of dismal performances. Local media outlets like The Philadelphia Inquirer splashed headlines heralding the draft pick as a "new dawn," with columnists praising Iverson's Georgetown exploits and predicting his speed would inject adrenaline into the lethargic Sixers. Fans, gathering in sports bars and call-in radio shows, buzzed with excitement—blue-collar workers and urban youth alike envisioning him as the gritty underdog to mirror their own resilient spirit, his tattoos and quiet swagger evoking a fresh, authentic edge absent since Charles Barkley's departure. Billboards and merchandise flew off shelves, the No. 3 jersey becoming a symbol of hope amid the franchise's 18-win nadir.

Yet, the hype carried undercurrents of pressure, immense for a 21-year-old tasked with single-handedly reversing fortunes in a town notorious for its unforgiving fandom—boos reserved for perceived slights, demands for immediate impact echoing through the CoreStates Spectrum. Emerging narratives painted Iverson as both savior and risk: supporters celebrated his potential to fuse street authenticity with pro excellence, a cultural bridge in a league tilting toward urban influences, while skeptics in national echoes worried his size and past troubles might crumble under Philly's scrutiny. As training camp anecdotes leaked—of his fearless drives and occasional tardiness—the city's pulse quickened, narratives solidifying around redemption and defiance, all building toward the electric unknown of his NBA debut.

As November 1, 1996, approached, the air in Philadelphia thickened with a palpable tension, the city's collective breath held in anticipation of Allen Iverson's NBA debut against the Milwaukee Bucks. Preseason glimpses had tantalized—flashes of his crossover leaving defenders in dust, pull-ups swishing through nets—but whispers of immaturity lingered, from tardy arrivals to clashes with Jerry Stackhouse, fueling narratives of a prodigy on the brink. Iverson, sequestered in his new world of luxury apartments and endless scrutiny, wrestled with the emotional grind: nights replaying film, body aching from practices that tested his limits, mind racing with the ghosts of Hampton's struggles. His mother Ann's visits grounded him, her pride a quiet anchor amid the hype, reminding him this was redemption incarnate—a chance to lift his family while etching his name in a league skeptical of his stature.

Media frenzy amplified the stakes; ESPN specials dissected his every move, fans packed the Spectrum for warm-ups, jerseys emblazoned with "Iverson" selling out as symbols of renewed faith. Philadelphia's blue-collar soul yearned for his grit to ignite a turnaround, yet pressure mounted like storm clouds—expectations to score, defend, lead, all while navigating the cultural tightrope of authenticity versus professionalism. Teammates eyed him warily, coaches drilled precision into his chaos, and the city buzzed with bets on his impact. As game day dawned, Iverson laced up in silence, heart pounding with the weight of destiny, the arena's roar awaiting the kid ready to unleash his storm.

The Rookie Who Bent The League

The lights of the Spectrum arena in Philadelphia hummed with anticipation on November 1, 1996, as the crowd settled in for the season opener against the Milwaukee Bucks. Allen Iverson, the wiry, tattooed rookie from Georgetown, fresh off being selected first overall in the draft, laced up his sneakers amid whispers of skepticism. At just 6 feet tall and 165 pounds, he didn't fit the mold of the prototypical NBA point guard—polished, poised, predictable. Instead, Iverson exploded onto the court like a bolt from the streets of Hampton, Virginia, his cornrows tight, his gaze unflinching. From the opening tip, his speed was a revelation, a blur that left defenders grasping at air. He darted through lanes with an audacious crossover, slicing past veterans like Vin Baker and Glenn Robinson as if they were mere cones in a drill.

Iverson's energy was infectious, a raw, unfiltered intensity that pulsed through every possession. He attacked the rim with fearless abandon, drawing fouls and converting tough layups, his quick release on jumpers catching the Bucks off guard. By halftime, he had already notched 18 points, his confidence swelling with each bucket. The crowd, a mix of blue-collar Philly fans hungry for a savior after years of mediocrity, erupted as he drained a three-pointer, his slight frame belying the power in his shot. Teammates like Clarence Weatherspoon fed off his vibe, but it was Iverson's solo runs—stealing the ball for a fast-break score, threading no-look passes—that announced a shift. This wasn't just skill; it was electricity, a hip-hop rhythm injected into the league's structured symphony.

Veterans on the sidelines exchanged glances, murmuring about this kid's audacity. Bucks coach Chris Ford later admitted the rookie's pace was unlike anything he'd prepared for, forcing adjustments mid-game. Iverson finished with 30 points on 12-of-19 shooting, adding six assists and a steal in 37 minutes, though the Sixers fell 111-103. It was a debut that shattered expectations, surpassing Jerry Stackhouse's 27-point mark from the previous year as the highest for a Sixer rookie in decades. But beyond the numbers, Iverson's presence signaled something deeper—a cultural jolt. His authenticity, from the tattoos peeking out under his jersey to his unapologetic swagger, made the league uncomfortable, hinting at debates to come about style versus substance. Fans saw a mirror to their own grit; the establishment saw a disruptor. In that one night, Iverson didn't just play; he bent the court to his will, proving small guards could dominate with heart over height.

The momentum from Iverson's debut carried into the next games like a freight train, shattering the league's preconceived notions of what a rookie point guard should be. In his second outing, against the defending champion Chicago Bulls on November 2, he managed 15 points despite a stifling defense, but it was his relentless pace that stood out—probing the Bulls' vaunted triangle offense with quick bursts that forced Michael Jordan and company to chase him relentlessly. Three days later, versus the Pistons, Iverson erupted for 24 points, grabbing seven rebounds and three steals, his crossover leaving defenders like Grant Hill in the dust, hinting at a style that blended streetball flair with NBA precision.

By his fourth game, on November 8 against the Celtics, Iverson's scoring burst hit a new peak: 32 points in 42 minutes, including 14-of-22 from the free-throw line, powering the Sixers to their first win of the season. His pace was unforgiving, turning transitions into personal showcases, where he'd accelerate from half-court to the rim in seconds, drawing fouls and energizing a struggling team. Teammates and coaches quickly pivoted; head coach Johnny Davis, initially cautious, made Iverson the offensive hub, logging him for over 40 minutes in multiple contests as the Sixers' record hovered around .500 early on.

Then came the explosion against the Knicks on November 12: 35 points, including five three-pointers, in a road victory that silenced Madison Square Garden. Iverson's bursts weren't just numbers; they disrupted defenses accustomed to taller, more methodical guards like Jason Kidd or Gary Payton. Veterans grumbled about his "unpredictable" style—too fast, too flashy—but Sixers fans saw a focal point emerging, a player who averaged over 22 points in his first eight games, outpacing expectations for a team that had won only 18 games the prior season. His quickness forced adjustments league-wide, with opponents doubling him off screens, yet he adapted, dishing assists and stealing possessions. Philadelphia's offense, once stagnant, now revolved around his energy, making him indispensable by mid-November. This rapid ascent didn't go unnoticed; whispers of "reckless" play mingled with awe, as Iverson's authenticity began to polarize the NBA's old guard.

Iverson's arrival shattered the archetype of the NBA point guard, a position long defined by orchestration and restraint—think John Stockton's precise passes or Magic Johnson's court vision. Instead, Iverson injected aggression into every dribble, treating the ball like a weapon forged in playground battles. His creativity wasn't scripted; it was instinctual, a whirlwind of ankle-breaking crossovers and hesitation moves that left defenders frozen, as if he'd rewritten the rules mid-play. In early games, like the November 16 clash with the Clippers, he scored 28 points with acrobatic layups and pull-up jumpers, his fearless shot-taking evident in contested threes that defied coaching manuals. Traditionalists balked at his 19.8 field goal attempts per game, labeling it reckless, but Iverson's 41.6% shooting masked his impact—averaging 23.5 points and 7.5 assists as a rookie, numbers that blended scoring punch with playmaking flair.

His aggression extended beyond offense; on defense, he averaged 2.1 steals, hounding ball-handlers with relentless pressure that turned turnovers into fast-break daggers. Coaches like Pat Riley, facing him in December, adjusted schemes to contain his speed, but Iverson's creativity shone through—threading behind-the-back passes or euro-stepping through traffic, innovations that echoed streetball but elevated the pro game. Fearless in the paint against giants like Shaquille O'Neal, he'd absorb contact for and-ones, his 7.2 free throw attempts per game a testament to his refusal to back down. This style polarized the league: veterans admired his heart but critiqued his shot selection, averaging 4.4 turnovers as he pushed boundaries. Yet, for young fans, Iverson represented liberation, proving small guards could dominate with audacity over size. By December, his influence rippled, inspiring copycats in AAU circuits, while the NBA grappled with a mold forever bent. His rookie stats underscored the shift, blending volume scoring with elite assists in a way that redefined the position's possibilities.

As Iverson's rookie campaign unfolded, established NBA players found themselves grappling with a phenomenon that defied their defensive instincts. His speed, a relentless, turbo-charged force, left veterans like Gary Payton chasing shadows, their lungs burning from the constant pursuit. One guard recounted the exhaustion of guarding him, admitting he was left drained in the showers post-game, pondering why this diminutive rookie could outpace seasoned pros so effortlessly. Frustration mounted as defenders, accustomed to containing taller, more deliberate guards, watched Iverson's crossover—a sharp, deceptive whip that snapped ankles and egos—render their footwork obsolete. Michael Jordan himself expressed disbelief, confessing he was "scared to death" of the move, noting no one had seen such a crossover before, and admitting he couldn't slide his feet fast enough to keep up. This mix of confusion and admiration rippled through the league; Charles Barkley marveled at Iverson's potential, calling him "disgusting" if he were taller, while others praised his warrior spirit, insisting he could score at will—40s, 50s, whatever he desired.

Yet, the reactions weren't uniformly positive. Some veterans voiced frustration over his unorthodox style, labeling it unpredictable and hard to scout, as it blended streetball improvisation with pro-level precision. In matchups against teams like the Lakers or Sonics, players like Shaquille O'Neal and Shawn Kemp showed visible irritation when Iverson blew past them for layups, his fearlessness clashing with the league's hierarchical norms. Admiration crept in, though, as legends recognized his impact: one noted you'd need peak conditioning to face him, and even then, fatigue was inevitable. Kobe Bryant later drew comparisons, preferring to concede points to a methodical scorer over Iverson's chaotic assault. This disbelief fueled early rivalries, with players like Tim Hardaway testing him in games, only to emerge humbled. Iverson's presence forced a reevaluation—small guards weren't just facilitators; they could humiliate giants. By mid-season, the league buzzed with stories of his exploits, his 23.5 points and 7.5 assists per game underscoring the stats behind the spectacle.

As Iverson's on-court exploits captivated audiences, his off-court persona ignited a firestorm of cultural debates that would redefine the NBA's image. From the outset of his rookie season, his cornrows—tightly woven braids that evoked street culture rather than the league's polished aesthetic—drew scrutiny, symbolizing a bold embrace of Black identity in a sport still dominated by conservative norms. He started sporting them early in 1996-97, a choice that, combined with his visible tattoos peeking from under his jersey, positioned him as an outlier. Veterans and executives whispered discomfort, viewing his ink—tributes to his Virginia roots and personal struggles—as markers of a "thug" image, a term laden with racial undertones that fueled media critiques. His baggy clothes, oversized jewelry, and hip-hop swagger off the court amplified this, clashing with the NBA's buttoned-up facade, where players like Michael Jordan embodied corporate appeal.

Yet, this authenticity resonated deeply with younger fans, particularly in urban communities, who saw Iverson as a mirror to their world—unfiltered, resilient, and defiant. Publications like Sports Illustrated ran pieces questioning whether his style undermined the game's professionalism, sparking broader discussions on race, class, and representation. League commissioner David Stern monitored the buzz, hinting at future policies to curb such expressions, while Philadelphia's blue-collar crowd embraced him as their own, chanting "A.I." amid the controversy. Iverson's refusal to conform turned him into a cultural flashpoint, bridging hip-hop and hoops; artists like Jay-Z name-dropped him in lyrics, and kids nationwide copied his look, from Reebok sneakers to arm sleeves. This tension highlighted the NBA's evolving identity, where Iverson's raw edge challenged the status quo, forcing the league to confront its discomfort with players who brought the streets courtside.

Iverson's scoring prowess escalated into legendary streaks that cemented his status as an unstoppable force, even against towering defenders who dwarfed his 6-foot frame. Towards the close of his rookie season in April 1997, he unleashed a five-game rampage of 40-plus point outings, a feat that shattered Wilt Chamberlain's rookie record of three consecutive such games and left the league in awe. It began against the Bulls with 44 points on efficient shooting, his quickness dismantling Chicago's vaunted defense as he attacked the rim relentlessly, drawing contact from bigger bodies like Luc Longley. The streak continued: 40 against the Nets, weaving through Patrick Ewing's reach; 46 versus the Heat, blowing past Alonzo Mourning for acrobatic finishes; 44 on the Bucks, outpacing Ervin Johnson's length with pull-ups; and a career-high 50 against the Cavaliers, humiliating Shawn Kemp and Bob Sura with crossovers that turned size into a liability. He capped it with 40 versus the Bullets, his averages over the span—44 points, 5 rebounds, 7 assists on 51% shooting—highlighting a blend of volume and efficiency rarely seen from a rookie.

This audacity against bigger defenders made Iverson instantly iconic, proving undersized guards could terrorize the paint with heart and handle. Veterans like Shaquille O'Neal, who faced him multiple times, marveled at his fearlessness, as Iverson absorbed elbows and charges to convert and-ones, his slight build belying a warrior's resolve. Fans dubbed him "The Answer," a nod to his solutions against any matchup, inspiring a generation to embrace aggression over altitude. Yet, the Sixers' losses in all five games underscored the team's woes, amplifying critiques of his shot volume. Still, these streaks transcended stats, etching Iverson as a cultural phenom who attacked the game's giants—literally and figuratively—with unyielding flair.

In the heart of a city known for its unyielding grit and blue-collar ethos, Allen Iverson found an immediate kindred spirit in Philadelphia's fans, who had endured years of mediocrity from a Sixers franchise that stumbled to just 18 wins the season before his arrival. From his electrifying debut, where he dropped 30 points amid roaring cheers at the Spectrum, Iverson injected life into a dormant team, transforming apathy into fervent hope. Fans, weary from the post-Barkley era of irrelevance, latched onto his raw energy—a tattooed, cornrowed underdog who mirrored their own street-smart resilience. Chants of "A.I." echoed through arenas as he slashed through defenses, his fearlessness resonating with a fanbase that prized authenticity over polish. By mid-season, attendance surged, with sellouts becoming commonplace as supporters packed venues to witness his scoring barrages, turning games into communal celebrations of defiance.

This bond formed swiftly, forged in Iverson's refusal to conform; Philly embraced him as their own, a symbol of the city's underdog spirit against the league's establishment. Local media hailed him as "The Answer," a moniker that captured the collective yearning for revival, while fans donned his jerseys and mimicked his style, from baggy shorts to arm sleeves. Even amid early controversies over his image, the connection deepened—fans defended him fiercely, seeing his background as a badge of honor rather than a blemish. Iverson reciprocated, crediting the city's tough love for fueling his drive, creating a symbiotic relationship that elevated the franchise from laughingstock to cultural touchstone. As the season progressed, this embrace solidified, with Iverson averaging crowds that hadn't been seen in years, his every crossover a spark for a fanbase starved for icons. In Philadelphia, he wasn't just a player; he was the pulse of a revival, binding a struggling team to its passionate city in ways that promised enduring loyalty.

As Iverson's rookie season intensified, tensions simmered across the league, birthing early rivalries that pitted his brash style against the NBA's entrenched guard hierarchy. His infamous declaration—"On the court, I don't respect anyone"—ignited backlash from veterans who viewed it as insolence, a direct challenge to the pecking order where rookies paid dues. Opposing guards, tasked with containing his explosive speed, often emerged frustrated and humbled. Take Nick Van Exel of the Lakers: in a December 1996 matchup, Iverson torched him for 30 points, his crossovers leaving Van Exel grasping, prompting Shaquille O'Neal to later recall the rookie's "oh s–t" dominance that demanded respect amid the rivalry. Gary Payton, the Sonics' defensive maestro, faced similar futility; in their February clash, Iverson dropped 35 points and seven assists, his pace exhausting Payton, who grumbled about the kid's unpredictability, fueling a budding antagonism between lockdown defenders and this uncontainable force.

Fellow rookies weren't spared: clashes with Stephon Marbury, the Timberwolves' point guard phenom, turned into personal battles, with Iverson outdueling him in head-to-heads—35 points in one, 28 in another—highlighting a rivalry of dueling egos among the draft class's elite. Even the Rookie Game in February 1997 stirred tension; Iverson's MVP performance (19 points, nine assists) overshadowed Kobe Bryant's dunk spectacle, leaving fans booing and whispers of resentment lingering. Veterans like Tim Hardaway and Jason Kidd attempted to school him in early encounters, but Iverson's fearless drives and scoring outbursts—averaging over 25 points against top guards—exposed their vulnerabilities, breeding admiration laced with irritation. These failures to corral him amplified league-wide discomfort, setting the stage for even greater confrontations. As March approached, one icon loomed largest: Michael Jordan, whose Bulls represented the ultimate test, a matchup brewing with electric anticipation.

As Iverson's dominance escalated, opposing teams shifted from strategic adjustments to outright physical warfare, desperate to blunt his speed and disrupt his rhythm. Veterans, sensing a threat to the league's established order, employed hard fouls and relentless pressure, treating the rookie like a pinball in a machine designed to bruise. In a February 1997 matchup against the Knicks, Charles Oakley—a notorious enforcer—delivered a brutal hip check that sent Iverson sprawling, a clear message to the audacious newcomer invading the paint. Oakley later downplayed it, but such tactics became commonplace; teams assigned bigger guards like Gary Payton or Derek Harper to body him full-court, hand-checking his every dribble under the era's permissive rules, aiming to wear down his 165-pound frame. Iverson's free throw attempts ballooned to 7.2 per game, a rookie high that reflected the contact he absorbed—544 total attempts over 76 games, often from flagrant hacks as he blew by defenders.

This physical targeting stirred controversy, with coaches like Pat Riley instructing players to "make him feel it" on drives, forcing Iverson to navigate elbows and screens that tested his resilience. Yet, he thrived amid the aggression, converting and-ones and drawing technicals on frustrated opponents, his quickness turning brute force into fouls. Personal fouls against him spiked in heated games, but Iverson's response—popping up unfazed, jawing back without complaint—only amplified his icon status. Teams like the Bulls and Lakers ramped up the pressure in rematches, double-teaming him at half-court to sap his energy, but these efforts often backfired, highlighting the league's struggle to contain a player who fed off adversity. As March loomed, one ultimate test awaited, where physicality would meet legend in a defining isolation.

As Iverson's rookie brilliance unfolded, the NBA's establishment—commissioned by David Stern's vision of a corporate-friendly league—bristled at his unyielding defiance of their sanitized image. His cornrows, adopted early in the 1996-97 season, became a symbol of resistance, evoking hip-hop authenticity that clashed with the polished personas of stars like Michael Jordan. Tattoos sprawling across his arms, once hidden under long sleeves in college, now boldly displayed, drew whispers of "thug" stereotypes from executives and media, who feared his style alienated suburban fans. Stern, intent on rebranding the NBA as upscale entertainment, viewed Iverson's baggy clothes, jewelry, and street vernacular as threats to marketability, sparking internal debates about enforcing conformity.

Commentary erupted in outlets like Sports Illustrated, where critics lambasted his "rebel" aesthetic as unprofessional, while others fascinated by his rawness hailed him as a cultural bridge between hoops and hip-hop. Iverson's refusal to alter his look—once delaying post-game interviews until his braids were perfect—intensified the criticism, positioning him as a lightning rod for racial undertones in discussions of player image. Amid the scrutiny, Iverson's on-court defiance mirrored his off-court ethos, setting the stage for a March showdown where his crossover would challenge not just a defender, but the league's very icons.

While Iverson's on-court fireworks drew headlines, it was his off-court style that ignited a cultural revolution among young fans, who saw in him a blueprint for unapologetic self-expression. Kids in urban playgrounds and suburban gyms alike mimicked his cornrows, a hairstyle he popularized during his rookie year, weaving them into a symbol of Black pride and defiance against the NBA's conservative norms. His swagger—evident in baggy shorts, oversized jerseys, and diamond chains—embodied hip-hop's influence, blending street authenticity with pro-level flair that resonated with a generation grappling with identity. Tattoos, once taboo in the league, became badges of honor under Iverson's lead; he sported over a dozen visible ones, inspiring youth to embrace body art as storytelling, from tributes to hometowns to personal mottos. His attitude, a mix of relentless confidence and vulnerability, spoke to misfits and underdogs, as he openly discussed his troubled past, turning perceived flaws into strengths.

This embrace shifted cultural norms profoundly, bridging basketball and hip-hop in ways that forced the NBA to evolve. Young fans flooded stores for Reebok sneakers and arm sleeves—another Iverson innovation—transforming league fashion from uniform to individualistic. Artists like Jadakiss and Jermaine Dupri referenced him in tracks, while AAU teams adopted his crossover and bravado, democratizing the game's aesthetic beyond elite circles. Iverson's influence extended to broader society, challenging racial stereotypes and empowering Black youth to own their narratives amid criticism. As his rookie season built toward climactic moments, this cultural ripple hinted at a league forever altered, with one impending matchup poised to etch his legacy in stone.

Iverson's rookie season unfolded like a highlight reel in real time, each game adding clips that electrified fans and media alike. From his debut against the Bucks, where he dazzled with a hesitation crossover on Glenn Robinson, leaving the veteran stumbling before drilling a mid-range jumper, Iverson's plays demanded instant replay. His speed turned fast breaks into spectacles—stealing inbound passes and gliding for reverse layups that seemed to defy gravity, his slight frame twisting mid-air to avoid blocks. In a November road win over the Knicks, he dropped 35 points, including a no-look pass in transition that set up Derrick Alston for a dunk, followed by his own step-back three that silenced the Garden crowd. These moments, captured on grainy VHS tapes traded among fans, built a burgeoning legend, with SportsCenter anchors dubbing him "The Answer" as his ankle-breakers and acrobatic finishes dominated nightly top-10 lists.

The energy surrounding his growing reel was palpable, a mix of awe and frenzy that rippled through locker rooms and living rooms. Teammates marveled at his audacity, like the December game against the Clippers where he euro-stepped past Loy Vaught for an and-one, absorbing contact with a grin. By late season, his five-game 40-point streak in April became mythic: 50 against the Cavaliers, weaving through Shawn Kemp for pull-ups and drives that left defenders in tatters. Kids on blacktops nationwide imitated his crossover, while the league buzzed with anticipation, his flair challenging norms. Yet, as March approached, whispers grew about a supreme test—a matchup where one play could immortalize him against the game's greatest.

Iverson's authenticity wasn't scripted; it erupted like a live wire, making his rise feel like a star birthing in real time amid the NBA's glossy arena lights. From the jump, his raw edge—tattoos mapping personal scars, cornrows channeling Hampton's streets, and a swagger borrowed from hip-hop cyphers—set him apart as unfiltered power incarnate. He didn't court approval; he demanded witness, his vulnerability laced with defiance, turning every press conference into a manifesto. "I'm me," he'd say simply, but in that declaration lay a revolution, challenging the league's airbrushed ideals with a gritty truth that resonated like a baseline thump.

Young fans felt it viscerally, seeing in Iverson a reflection of their own unpolished worlds—authentic, imperfect, invincible. His style spread like wildfire: kids adopting arm sleeves to mimic his on-court armor, braids becoming badges of rebellion, and oversized jerseys a uniform for the underrepresented. This wasn't mere fashion; it was empowerment, a powerful assertion that Black culture belonged at the game's forefront, unapologetic and dominant. The establishment squirmed, but Iverson's unfiltered presence amplified his stardom, his every crossover a metaphor for breaking barriers. As his rookie year hurtled forward, this raw force built an aura of inevitability, positioning him as the disruptor ready to challenge the throne. With March's Bulls matchup looming, the stage was set for a moment that would crystallize his power against the ultimate icon.

As Iverson's rookie season barreled through winter into spring, a compelling narrative coalesced around him, transforming the Sixers' guard into the league's most polarizing storyline. Tension mounted with each game, as his scoring streaks—culminating in that blistering April run of five straight 40-point explosions—clashed with the team's dismal 22-60 record, amplifying critiques of his individualism amid collective failure. Excitement pulsed through arenas, where fans packed seats to witness his electric bursts, his crossover becoming a whispered legend, a move that humiliated defenders and ignited debates on style versus strategy. Media outlets dissected his every move, from Sports Illustrated profiles probing his "rebel" ethos to ESPN highlights looping his acrobatic drives, building a mythos of the undersized warrior defying giants.

Yet, beneath the thrill lurked unease—the league's old guard, including coaches like Phil Jackson, schemed to neutralize him, while cultural commentators grappled with his influence on youth, his braids and tattoos sparking imitation waves that redefined NBA fashion from corporate sleek to street authentic. Anticipation swelled as rivalries sharpened; early skirmishes with guards like Gary Payton foreshadowed greater battles, each encounter heightening the stakes. By March, the buzz centered on an impending clash with the Bulls, where Iverson's audacity would face the ultimate benchmark. Whispers circulated: Could this rookie truly challenge the GOAT? The stage was set at

CoreStates Center, the air thick with expectancy, as Iverson isolated at the top of the key, the moment hanging like a promise of immortality.

The buildup to March 12, 1997, crackled with an electric undercurrent, as the Philadelphia 76ers prepared to host the defending champion Chicago Bulls at the CoreStates Center. The Sixers, mired in a 16-46 slump, faced a juggernaut Bulls squad boasting a 55-8 record, led by the indomitable Michael Jordan, whose aura of invincibility loomed like a shadow over the league. Whispers had circulated for weeks: Could this brash rookie, with his street-honed flair and unyielding confidence, truly test the GOAT? Iverson, averaging 23.5 points and 7.5 assists amid a season of cultural upheaval, embodied the tension—his tattoos, braids, and defiant swagger a stark contrast to Jordan's polished empire. Fans packed the arena, a sea of blue and red buzzing with anticipation, sensing a generational clash that transcended the scoreboard.

As tip-off neared, the narrative peaked: Iverson's scoring streaks and fearless drives had already bent defenses, but this matchup promised immortality. Jordan, at 34, represented the establishment Iverson challenged—corporate poise versus raw authenticity. Teammates like Jerry Stackhouse fed off the energy, while coaches braced for a high-stakes duel. The game unfolded intensely, a back-and-forth battle where Iverson's quickness pierced Chicago's triangle, outscoring Jordan 37 to 23 on efficient shooting. Late in the third quarter, with the score tight, Iverson called for the isolation at the top of the key, Jordan guarding him closely, the crowd rising in unison. The ball bounced, time slowed, and the league held its breath for what would become legend.

The 76ers Build The AI Era

On March 12, 1997, in the electric confines of Philadelphia's CoreStates Center, the NBA witnessed a seismic shift disguised as a single dribble. The Philadelphia 76ers, mired in a rebuilding haze, trailed the defending champion Chicago Bulls late in the third quarter. Rookie Allen Iverson, the wiry 6-foot guard from Georgetown with cornrows and tattoos that screamed defiance, isolated at the top of the key. Michael Jordan, the undisputed king of the league at 34, switched onto him after a screen—Phil Jackson's call echoing from the Bulls' bench. Iverson, ball in his right hand, sized up his idol with a predator's calm. He jabbed right, a subtle hesitation that froze Jordan in anticipation, the veteran's feet planted as if bracing for the drive. Then came the explosion: Iverson snapped the ball left with a vicious crossover dribble, so quick it blurred the line between skill and sorcery. Jordan lunged desperately, his Airness stumbling awkwardly as his ankles betrayed him, nearly touching the hardwood.

The arena detonated. Over 20,000 fans leaped from their seats, a roar cascading through the building like thunder, shaking the rafters and drowning out the referees' whistles. Iverson didn't hesitate—he pulled up smoothly for the mid-range jumper, swishing it clean as the crowd's frenzy peaked. It wasn't just a bucket in a 108-104 loss; it was heresy. A 21-year-old rookie had baptized the GOAT, dropping 37 points on 15-of-23 shooting while holding Jordan to 23 on inefficient 9-of-24. The play's cultural weight was immediate and profound: Iverson's crossover embodied the raw, street-ball ethos clashing with Jordan's polished corporate iconography, a symbol of hip-hop's infiltration into the NBA's buttoned-up world. Overnight, replays flooded ESPN, igniting debates from barbershops to boardrooms. For the league, it shattered perceptions of Iverson as a mere scoring flash—here was a phenom with handles that could humble legends. For the Sixers, languishing at 22-60 that season, the moment was a revelation. No longer could they view Iverson as a risky lottery pick; this spark demanded they reimagine their franchise around him, planting the seeds for an era where his audacity would redefine Philadelphia basketball. The AI revolution had begun, forcing organizational pivots that would echo for years.

The shockwaves from Iverson's crossover rippled far beyond the CoreStates Center that night, eliciting reactions that underscored the play's transformative power. Michael Jordan, ever the competitor, addressed the moment post-game with a mix of grace and candor, telling reporters that the rookie had executed "a great move" and admitting, "He got me pretty good." His words carried weight—here was the league's deity acknowledging a mortal's audacity, a rare concession that humanized Jordan while elevating Iverson. Iverson, for his part, revealed his lingering reverence, approaching Jordan after the buzzer to confess, "You were my hero," only for Jordan to quip back, "I couldn't have been too much of a hero if you crossed me like that." The exchange highlighted the tension between admiration and rivalry, with other players like Bulls teammate Scottie Pippen noting Iverson's fearlessness as a sign of emerging talent that could reshape matchups.

Commentators amplified the frenzy, with NBC's broadcast crew gasping in real-time—"Oh, he crossed him over!"—as replays looped endlessly on SportsCenter the next day. Analysts like Hubie Brown labeled it a "changing of the guard," praising Iverson's handles as revolutionary, while print media from The Philadelphia Inquirer to Sports Illustrated dissected the play as emblematic of the NBA's evolving guard play, blending street-ball flair with pro precision. Fans, both in the arena and nationwide, erupted in a collective gasp followed by euphoria; Philadelphia loyalists saw it as validation of their city's grit, while Bulls supporters debated it heatedly in bars and online forums, then nascent. The moment's virality—fueled by highlight reels and word-of-mouth—sparked barbershop arguments from coast to coast, with many viewing Iverson not as a fluke but a harbinger of disruption.

This wasn't mere rookie hype; the crossover signaled Iverson as a generational disruptor, shattering the mold of what a star guard could be. Where Jordan represented polished excellence and corporate appeal, Iverson embodied raw authenticity—cornrows, tattoos, and unapologetic swagger—that challenged the league's conservative image. It redefined his ceiling from promising scorer to potential icon, forcing skeptics to confront his ability to humble legends and infuse the game with hip-hop's rebellious energy. For the Sixers, it crystallized the need to build around this force, as national attention surged, hinting at a franchise rebirth rooted in Iverson's defiant brilliance. The play didn't just score points; it ignited a cultural recalibration, paving the way for Iverson's ascent as the NBA's next transformative figure.

In the aftermath of Iverson's audacious crossover, the Philadelphia 76ers' front office faced a reckoning. The 1996-97 season had ended in dismal fashion—a 22-60 record under head coach Johnny Davis, plagued by inconsistent play and a lack of cohesion. Yet, amid the rubble, Iverson's 23.5 points per game and that electrifying moment against Jordan illuminated his untapped potential. No longer could the organization treat him as a high-risk experiment; the crossover had exposed his ability to command the spotlight, drawing national intrigue to a franchise starved for relevance since the Julius Erving era. Team president Pat Croce, who had taken the reins in 1996 with a mandate to revitalize the stagnant operation, recognized the imperative: Iverson wasn't just a player—he was the nucleus around which a new identity must orbit.

Swift action followed. In May 1997, just weeks after the season's close, the Sixers fired Davis, their fifth coach in six years, signaling an end to the carousel of instability. They lured Larry Brown from the Indiana Pacers, a defensive-minded tactician with a Hall of Fame pedigree, to steer the ship. Brown's arrival marked a philosophical pivot: away from scattershot talent accumulation toward a deliberate build centered on Iverson's offensive wizardry. On draft night that June, the team traded scoring guard Jerry Stackhouse—once seen as a co-star—to the Detroit Pistons for defensive stalwarts Theo Ratliff and Aaron McKie, fortifying the roster with grit to complement Iverson's flair. This move underscored the commitment: Stackhouse's departure cleared the lane for Iverson to evolve from point guard to scoring guard, unleashing his crossover artistry without overlap.

Internally, the shifts stirred optimism. Croce's energetic leadership infused the organization with a street-smart vibe that mirrored Iverson's own, while Brown's no-nonsense approach promised discipline. Fans, long disillusioned by lottery purgatory, began to buy in, sensing a cultural alignment between the city's blue-collar ethos and Iverson's unyielding drive. The crossover had been the catalyst, but these maneuvers solidified the vision—an "AI era" where Philadelphia basketball would rise on the shoulders of its defiant icon, setting the stage for contention and a redefined franchise soul.

As the 76ers committed to centering their franchise on Allen Iverson, internal debates simmered in the front office, pitting traditional basketball orthodoxy against the rookie's unbridled creativity. Pat Croce, the charismatic president with a background in physical therapy and motivational speaking, championed Iverson's raw energy as the key to revitalizing a dormant fanbase, viewing his aggression as a cultural magnet for Philadelphia's tough, working-class identity. Yet, skepticism lingered among executives and scouts who questioned whether Iverson's freelance style—marked by high-volume shooting, dazzling crossovers, and occasional turnovers—could sustain a winning team without rigid structure. "He's a Ferrari," one anonymous source from the era later reflected in interviews, "but does he need a racetrack or just open road?" The crux of the discussions revolved around this: impose a conventional system to curb his instincts, or craft a roster that amplified his improvisational genius?

Larry Brown's hiring intensified these deliberations. Known for his defensive rigor and emphasis on fundamentals from stints with the Clippers and Pacers, Brown arrived with a blueprint that clashed with Iverson's improvisational ethos. Early meetings with Croce and newly appointed general manager Billy King, who joined in 1997, revealed fractures—Brown advocated for surrounding Iverson with disciplined role players to mitigate his defensive lapses and ball-dominant tendencies, while others worried that over-structuring might dull his edge, the very spark that had crossed over Jordan. Debates extended to scouting reports: Should they prioritize traditional big men for pick-and-roll synergy, or athletic wings to match Iverson's pace? The 1997 draft and trades reflected a compromise, adding versatile pieces like Tim Thomas for offensive flexibility, but the underlying tension foreshadowed future conflicts.

These early conversations underscored a broader NBA shift, as the league grappled with hip-hop-influenced talents challenging the post-Jordan paradigm. For the Sixers, resolving the debate meant betting on adaptation—tailoring the roster to Iverson's aggression while layering in Brown's structure. By the 1997-98 season, with a 31-51 record showing incremental progress, the front office's evolving consensus leaned toward hybridization: empower Iverson's creativity with defensive anchors, laying groundwork for his maturation into a leader capable of carrying the franchise toward contention. This internal push-pull not only shaped team strategy but mirrored Philadelphia's own identity crisis, transforming Iverson from enigma to cornerstone.

As the 1997-98 season unfolded, the 76ers' initial efforts to shoehorn Allen Iverson into the archetype of a conventional point guard exposed the limitations of forcing his boundless creativity into a distributor's mold. Under Larry Brown, fresh off his Pacers tenure, Iverson clashed with the coach's insistence on structured play—running precise sets, prioritizing assists over isolation heroics, and tempering his high-risk crossovers with team-oriented fundamentals. Iverson's rookie year had seen him average 7.5 assists but also lead the league in turnovers at 4.4, a statistic that frustrated executives who envisioned him as a floor general in the vein of Isiah Thomas or Magic Johnson. Brown's early practices became battlegrounds, with Iverson's improvisational flair—rooted in

Hampton's playgrounds and Georgetown's up-tempo system—chafing against the coach's demands for discipline, leading to public spats and whispers of incompatibility.

Yet, amid the friction, a pivotal shift emerged by the lockout-shortened 1998-99 campaign. Brown, recognizing Iverson's scoring instincts as his superpower, repositioned him from point guard to shooting guard, a move that liberated his aggression without the burden of primary ball-handling. The acquisition of steady point guard Eric Snow via trade from the Cavaliers in January 1998 provided the perfect complement, allowing Snow to orchestrate the offense while Iverson roamed as a lethal off-ball threat and isolation artist. This adjustment not only reduced Iverson's turnovers but amplified his scoring, jumping from 22.0 points per game in 1997-98 to 26.8 the following season, tops in the league. The front office, led by Pat Croce and Billy King, endorsed the change, signaling a broader organizational pivot: rather than taming Iverson's street-ball ethos, they leaned into it, surrounding him with defensive-minded role players like George Lynch and Theo Ratliff to mask his size and occasional lapses.

This embrace transformed the Sixers' identity, aligning with Philadelphia's underdog spirit and Iverson's cultural resonance. No longer viewed as a problem to fix, his style became the franchise's engine, fostering a gritty, fast-paced brand that propelled them to a 28-22 record in 1999 and their first playoff berth since 1991. The shift wasn't seamless—tensions with Brown persisted—but it marked the dawn of mutual adaptation, where Iverson's defiance fueled a resurgence, setting the table for deeper postseason runs and his evolution into an MVP contender.

With the positional shift solidifying Allen Iverson as the offensive fulcrum, the 76ers' front office, under general manager Billy King and coach Larry Brown, intensified their pursuit of complementary pieces—rugged defenders, relentless rebounders, and athletic runners who could thrive in transition without stealing the spotlight. The strategy was clear: insulate Iverson's defensive vulnerabilities, where his 6-foot frame and gambling style often left gaps, by assembling a roster of blue-collar enforcers. This hunt began in earnest during the 1998 offseason, when they signed free agent forward George Lynch, a tenacious wing from North Carolina whose 2.0 steals and 6.5 rebounds per game in the lockout-shortened 1998-99 season provided the grit to mask Iverson's lapses and fuel fast breaks. They also traded young forward Tim Thomas and center Scott Williams to Milwaukee for power forward Tyrone Hill, a bruising rebounder who averaged 7.3 boards that year, anchoring the paint and allowing Iverson to push the pace off misses.

The acquisitions continued into 1999-2000, with the addition of center Todd MacCulloch in the draft for depth and a mid-season three-team deal that brought versatile forward Toni Kukoč from Chicago, though his scoring role was secondary to the defensive core. Theo Ratliff, already a fixture, emerged as a rim-protecting force with 3.0 blocks per game, enabling Iverson to roam freely and lead the league in steals at 2.1. Aaron McKie, versatile off the bench, added 1.3 steals, while Eric Snow's steady facilitation (7.6 assists) ensured the ball found Iverson in rhythm. The pinnacle came in February 2001, when King orchestrated a blockbuster: sending the injured Ratliff, Kukoč, and Nazr Mohammed to Atlanta for Dikembe Mutombo, the ultimate defensive anchor whose 12.4

rebounds and 2.5 blocks per game transformed the frontcourt into a fortress. These moves coalesced into a unit that ranked fifth in defensive rating, unleashing Iverson's scoring fury—he averaged 31.1 points in 2000-01—while the team's 56-26 record signaled a contender built for his brilliance. Philadelphia's investment in these unsung heroes not only amplified Iverson's creativity but embodied the city's resilient ethos, turning a once-fragile roster into a symphony of support.

Even as the 76ers assembled defensive pieces around Allen Iverson, the early years of the build exposed deep fissures, with roster imbalances amplifying the friction of molding a team to his unprecedented style. The 1997-98 season, Brown's first, saw modest gains—a 31-51 record, up from the prior year's nadir—but the squad's overreliance on Iverson's scoring (26.8 points per game) highlighted glaring weaknesses. Without a reliable second option, Iverson's high-usage approach led the league in minutes (41.5) and turnovers (3.7), straining the offense as role players like Derrick Coleman and Clarence Weatherspoon faltered in consistency, their rebounding unable to offset defensive lapses in a league favoring size and structure. The lockout-shortened 1998-99 campaign brought a 28-22 mark and playoff berth, yet imbalances persisted: the team's gritty defense ranked top-10, but offensive stagnation forced Iverson into hero ball, exacerbating fatigue and inefficiency.

Internal tensions boiled over, particularly between Iverson and Brown, whose authoritarian coaching clashed with the guard's freewheeling ethos. Brown's demands for punctuality and practice intensity met resistance from Iverson, whose late nights and street-rooted independence symbolized a broader cultural rift—hip-hop defiance versus old-school discipline. A December 1999 in-game blowup epitomized the strife, with Iverson benched after arguing strategy, fueling rumors of trades and front-office headaches. Pat Croce mediated, but the friction underscored the challenge of building around a star whose crossover artistry and aggression defied convention—too small for traditional guard duties, too creative for rigid schemes. These struggles tested the organization's resolve, as Philadelphia fans oscillated between adoration and frustration, witnessing a franchise in flux. Yet, amid the chaos, seeds of synergy emerged, with Iverson's maturation hinting at the MVP-level leap ahead.

The arrival of Larry Brown in May 1997 marked a watershed moment for the 76ers, injecting a dose of veteran authority into a franchise desperate for direction after another lottery-bound season. Fresh from guiding the Indiana Pacers to back-to-back Eastern Conference Finals, Brown brought a Hall of Fame resume built on defensive tenacity and meticulous fundamentals—principles honed through stints with the Clippers, Spurs, and college ranks. Pat Croce, sensing Brown's track record could harness Iverson's raw talent, lured him with a vision of rebuilding around the young guard's explosiveness. Yet, from the outset, Brown's hiring ignited a philosophical collision: his insistence on structured play, team-first discipline, and relentless practice clashed with Iverson's instinctive freedom, a style forged in Virginia's playgrounds where creativity trumped convention.

This tension manifested immediately in training camp, where Brown's demands for punctuality and precision grated against Iverson's nocturnal habits and improvisational flair. Iverson, averaging 26.8 points but leading in turnovers, embodied hip-hop's unfiltered rebellion—cornrows flying as he darted through defenses with crossovers that defied schematics. Brown, the old-school taskmaster, viewed such individualism as inefficiency, pushing for a system that prioritized ball movement and defensive rotations over isolation heroics. Public spats ensued, with Brown benching Iverson during games and criticizing his shot selection, while Iverson chafed at the perceived micromanagement, fueling trade rumors and front-office anxiety. The friction highlighted broader NBA evolutions, as Brown's traditionalism confronted the league's shifting guard toward athletic, culturally resonant stars like Iverson, whose authenticity resonated with Philadelphia's gritty underclass.

Despite the volatility, this clash laid bare the potential for synergy—if Iverson could adapt without losing his edge, and Brown could flex his rigidity. By the 1999-2000 season, incremental compromises emerged, with Brown repositioning Iverson at shooting guard to unleash his scoring while bolstering the defense around him. The philosophical divide, though enduring, became the crucible for Iverson's growth, transforming early discord into the foundation of a Finals run and his MVP trajectory.

The early clashes between Allen Iverson and Larry Brown were as inevitable as they were explosive, a collision of worlds that exposed the fault lines in the NBA's evolving landscape. From the jump, Brown's regimented practices—demanding early arrivals, repetitive drills, and a focus on team defense—rubbed against Iverson's improvisational spirit, bred from late-night pickup games where survival meant outcreating opponents. Iverson, often arriving late or skipping sessions altogether, viewed Brown's rules as chains on his natural game, stifling the very flair that had crossed over Jordan. Brown, in turn, saw Iverson's habits as selfish, a lack of commitment that undermined the collective grind he prized from his own blue-collar roots in Long Beach, New York, and decades coaching in the league's more conservative eras.

Arguments flared publicly and privately. In one infamous 1997 practice, Brown halted drills to berate Iverson for erratic shot selection, barking that his isolation plays were "street ball, not pro ball," while Iverson fired back, defending his instincts as the reason fans packed the arena. Misunderstandings deepened the rift: Brown misinterpreted Iverson's cornrows and tattoos as symbols of rebellion against authority, overlooking their cultural significance in hip-hop's narrative of resilience. Iverson perceived Brown's criticisms as racial undertones, an old-guard white coach trying to "tame" a Black star from the hood, echoing broader societal tensions.

What both men represented amplified the drama. Brown embodied the NBA's traditional ethos—structure, sacrifice, and the ghosts of Red Auerbach and Dean Smith—while Iverson personified the league's hip-hop infusion, a defiant icon for a generation rejecting conformity. These battles, though bruising, forced mutual introspection, hinting at the alchemy that could forge a contender from their discord. By 1999, as the Sixers clawed toward relevance, the clashes began yielding to uneasy respect, laying the groundwork for Iverson's transcendent rise.

Amid the fireworks of their early confrontations, the battles between Allen Iverson and Larry Brown gradually forged a bond of mutual respect, transforming raw discord into the bedrock of the Sixers' resurgence. What began as ideological warfare—Brown's unyielding structure versus Iverson's untamed freedom—evolved through exhaustive dialogues and shared setbacks. Brown, initially exasperated by Iverson's tardiness and individualism, came to appreciate the guard's unrelenting work ethic once he peeled back the layers, recognizing that Iverson's defiance stemmed from a survival instinct honed in poverty-stricken Newport News. Iverson, in turn, began to see Brown's criticisms not as attacks but as tough love from a coach who had molded champions, his demands a pathway to unlocking collective potential rather than personal suppression.

This deepening respect manifested in subtle shifts. By the 1999-2000 season, Brown adjusted his schemes to spotlight Iverson's scoring, while Iverson embraced defensive responsibilities, leading the league in steals and minutes. Their public reconciliation—Brown praising Iverson's heart in press conferences, Iverson crediting the coach for his growth—signaled a partnership that resonated with Philadelphia's blue-collar soul, where grit and grind trumped polish. The tension, once a liability, became the AI era's foundation: it instilled discipline without extinguishing Iverson's fire, fostering a roster that blended street-ball audacity with professional rigor.

This alchemy propelled the Sixers from lottery dwellers to Eastern Conference contenders, with a 49-33 record in 2000 marking their ascent. Iverson's MVP-caliber play—31.1 points, 4.6 assists—emerged from this crucible, embodying a franchise identity reborn in hip-hop defiance and old-school tenacity. Philadelphia's fans, emotionally invested in the saga, rallied behind the duo, turning the Spectrum into a fortress of loyalty. The battles didn't vanish, but they built an era where Iverson's iconoclasm thrived, setting the stage for Finals glory and cultural immortality.

As Allen Iverson's game matured under Larry Brown's tutelage, NBA fans and media recalibrated their gaze on Philadelphia, transforming the Sixers from a punchline of perennial underachievement into symbols of unyielding grit. Early skepticism—rooted in Iverson's polarizing image as a tattooed, cornrowed disruptor who embodied hip-hop's edge—gave way to fascination as the team's record improved, climbing from 31-51 in 1997-98 to 49-33 by 1999-2000, culminating in a second-round playoff exit against the Pacers. National outlets like Sports Illustrated and ESPN began framing the Sixers not as a mismatched collection of talent but as underdogs channeling Philly's blue-collar ethos, with Iverson's relentless drives and crossovers mirroring the city's defiant spirit against powerhouse franchises.

Fans nationwide latched onto this narrative, Iverson's jerseys becoming ubiquitous from urban playgrounds to suburban malls, his 31.1 points per game in 2000-01 drawing comparisons to undersized legends like Isiah Thomas but with a cultural twist that appealed to a younger, diverse audience. Media perceptions shifted dramatically during the 2001 playoffs, where the Sixers' improbable run to the Finals—dispatching the Pacers, Raptors, and Bucks—painted Philadelphia as basketball's resilient heart, a franchise reborn through Iverson's evolution from flashy rookie to MVP frontrunner. Outlets highlighted the team's defensive tenacity and Iverson's leadership, even amid controversies like the infamous "practice" rant in 2002, later contextualized as grief-fueled rather than flippant. This reevaluation amplified Philadelphia's emotional stake, turning local loyalty into national intrigue, as the AI era solidified the Sixers' identity as cultural trailblazers poised for superstardom.

As Allen Iverson's star ascended, he transcended basketball to become the pulsating heartbeat of Philadelphia, a city that gazed into his defiant spirit and recognized its own reflection. Philly, forged in the fires of industrial grit and revolutionary fervor, had long embraced underdogs—blue-collar workers battling economic decline, neighborhoods scarred by poverty and racial strife. Iverson, hailing from Hampton's rough streets, embodied that ethos: a 6-foot survivor who had endured incarceration as a teen, emerging with unapologetic tattoos, cornrows, and a crossover that screamed rebellion. His refusal to conform—to the NBA's corporate polish or critics' expectations—mirrored the city's own history of defiance, from the Liberty Bell's crack to the MOVE bombing's scars.

Fans poured their emotional investment into him, packing the First Union Center with a fervor absent since Dr. J's heyday. Attendance surged from 14,000 per game in 1997 to over 20,000 by 2001, as working-class Philadelphians saw in Iverson's relentless drives their daily hustle, his trash-talk echoing their street-smart resilience. The franchise's marketing pivot amplified this bond, dubbing it the "AI era" with campaigns spotlighting his hip-hop ties—Reebok commercials blending courtside flair with urban anthems, merchandise flying off shelves in North Philly barbershops. National attention followed, with outlets dubbing him "The Answer" for a city seeking redemption after decades of sports heartbreak.

This symbiosis transformed the Sixers' identity, from lottery laughingstock to cultural vanguard, as Iverson's authenticity drew diverse crowds, bridging racial divides in a segregated town. His evolution fueled long-term retooling, with the organization betting on his leadership, laying foundations for an MVP season where his heart would propel them to unforeseen heights.

The Philadelphia 76ers' roster transformation unfolded gradually, a deliberate pivot from offensive-minded inconsistency to a gritty, defensive juggernaut designed to amplify Allen Iverson's scoring prowess. In the wake of the 1996-97 debacle, general manager Billy King and coach Larry Brown initiated the overhaul with a June 1997 trade, shipping Jerry Stackhouse—once envisioned as a co-star—to Detroit for defensive anchors Theo Ratliff and Aaron McKie. Ratliff, a shot-blocking force averaging 3.5 blocks per game in 1997-98, fortified the paint, while McKie's versatility (1.4 steals off the bench) provided perimeter tenacity, allowing Iverson to gamble without exposing the team. This move improved their defensive rating from 111.4 (26th in the league) in 1996-97 to 105.4 the following year.

By 1998, the blueprint deepened with the acquisition of point guard Eric Snow from Seattle in January, whose steady facilitation (7.1 assists in 1998-99) freed Iverson from primary playmaking duties, and free agent forward George Lynch, a rebounding hound averaging 6.5 boards. A summer trade for Tyrone Hill added bruising physicality, his 9.0 rebounds per game in 1998-99 embodying the emerging "no layups" ethos. The lockout-shortened season saw the defensive rating plummet to 97.6, ranking fifth league-wide, as the unit's collective grit—emphasizing rebounds, steals, and blocks—masked Iverson's size limitations.

The crescendo came in February 2001, trading Ratliff, Toni Kukoč, and Nazr Mohammed to Atlanta for Dikembe Mutombo, the Defensive Player of the Year whose 2.7 blocks and 13.5 rebounds transformed the frontcourt into an impenetrable wall. This roster, now a symphony of unsung enforcers like Matt Geiger and Raja Bell, posted a 98.9 defensive rating, propelling a 56-26 record. Iverson's offensive brilliance—31.1 points per game—thrived amid the bruising support, turning the Sixers into Eastern Conference elites and laying the MVP groundwork.

The Philadelphia 76ers' front office, under the steady hands of president Pat Croce and general manager Billy King, embodied a philosophy of patient reconstruction, steadfastly refusing the allure of quick-fix superstars or hasty overhauls that plagued other rebuilding teams. In an era where big-market franchises chased marquee free agents, the Sixers opted for methodical trades and draft picks, prioritizing pieces that could endure the physical toll of Iverson's high-octane style. Croce, with his motivational flair, and King, a former assistant under Brown, understood that Iverson's brilliance demanded a supporting cast built for longevity, not flash—defenders who could rebound, rotate, and run without crumbling under his relentless pace.

This gradual approach began post-1997 draft, when they traded Jerry Stackhouse, a scoring duplicate, to Detroit for Theo Ratliff's rim protection and Aaron McKie's perimeter versatility, improving defensive efficiency without sacrificing future assets. They eschewed splashy signings, instead claiming Eric Snow off waivers in 1998, a low-risk move that yielded a reliable facilitator to share ball-handling duties. The 1998 trade for Tyrone Hill brought rebounding muscle, while avoiding cap-crippling contracts. Even as the team hovered around .500 in the lockout year, the front office resisted panic, focusing on chemistry over star power.

By 2000, this patience paid dividends, with the roster's cohesion allowing Iverson to average 28.4 points amid a 49-33 campaign. The crowning stroke came in February 2001: trading Ratliff—now injured—for Dikembe Mutombo, a calculated swap that fortified the interior without gutting the core. This refusal of shortcuts cultivated a bruising, resilient unit, climbing from lottery obscurity to 56 wins, proving that sustainable building around Iverson's defiance could forge a contender. Philadelphia's investment mirrored its city's ethos—gritty, unyielding, and built to last.

By the dawn of the 2000-01 season, the Philadelphia 76ers had fully embraced the construction of the AI era, a holistic transformation that wove together structural fortitude, cultural resonance, and emotional fervor. Structurally, the roster had coalesced into a defensive powerhouse, with Dikembe Mutombo's arrival sealing the paint and veterans like Eric Snow and Aaron McKie providing the glue for Iverson's offensive explosions. The team's 56-26 record, a franchise high since 1985-86, reflected Larry Brown's system finally syncing with Iverson's improvisational genius, yielding a top-five defense that propelled them to the Eastern Conference's top seed.

Culturally, the franchise leaned into Iverson's hip-hop-infused identity, marketing campaigns blasting "The Answer" across billboards and merchandise, while his Reebok line and crossover appeal drew a new generation of fans, blending street culture with NBA lore. Emotionally, Philadelphia's investment reached fever pitch—the city's underdog soul mirrored in Iverson's battles, from courtroom scars to on-court triumphs, forging an unbreakable bond. Fans filled the First Union Center, chanting his name as he averaged 31.1 points, leading the league in scoring and steals en route to his first MVP award. This embrace wasn't mere strategy; it was a covenant, positioning Iverson as the icon ready to storm the Finals and etch his name among the immortals, his ascent to superstardom now inevitable.

2001: The MVP Season

Stepping into their roles with precision and grit. Eric Snow, the steady point guard, orchestrated the offense with unflashy efficiency, while Aaron McKie, the versatile swingman who would later earn Sixth Man of the Year honors, provided scoring punch off the bench. George Lynch and Tyrone Hill anchored the frontcourt with relentless rebounding and physicality, complementing Theo Ratliff's shot-blocking prowess at center. This wasn't a team of superstars but of specialists, each piece fitting into Larry Brown's puzzle of suffocating defense and opportunistic offense. The Sixers' identity had sharpened over the offseason: no longer just Iverson's show, but a collective force where his scoring explosions were amplified by a roster committed to the grind. Renewed confidence stemmed from the previous year's playoff run, where they pushed the Indiana Pacers to six games, proving they could hang with the East's elite. Practices buzzed with intensity, Brown's demanding style now embraced rather than resisted, fostering a belief that this season could etch their names in history. Iverson, evolving as a leader, bought in fully, his work ethic inspiring teammates to match his fire. As the wins piled up—ten in a row to start, including blowouts over the Knicks and Raptors—the locker room hummed with quiet conviction. Philadelphia, a city that revered underdogs, saw in this squad a reflection of its own blue-collar ethos. Fans chanted "M-V-P" early, sensing Iverson's dominance could propel them beyond regular-season success. The national media, once skeptical, began taking notice, whispering about a potential Finals berth. For the first time in nearly two decades, the Sixers carried the weight of expectation, not burden, but fuel for something historic—a run that would redefine resilience in the NBA.

As the season unfolded, Allen Iverson emerged not just as the Sixers' scoring machine but as an emotionally evolved force, his once-turbulent energy now channeled with precision and purpose. Entering his fifth year, Iverson had confronted the demons of his early career—off-court distractions, clashes with authority, and the weight of being Philadelphia's prodigal son—and transformed them into fuel for growth. The summer of 2000 marked a turning point; rumors of trades swirled, but Iverson recommitted, shedding the defiant posture that had defined his rookie seasons for a more introspective focus. He arrived at training camp leaner, sharper, his workouts legendary for their intensity, often extending late into the night as he honed crossovers and mid-range jumpers. This wasn't the Iverson who bristled at Larry Brown's critiques; instead, he absorbed them, recognizing that leadership demanded more than individual brilliance—it required vulnerability and trust.

On the court, his evolution manifested in subtle yet profound ways. Iverson's assists ticked up to 4.6 per game, a career high at the time, as he orchestrated pick-and-rolls with Ratliff and trusted Snow to initiate sets, allowing him to conserve energy for clutch moments. Teammates noticed the shift: McKie later recalled how Iverson's encouragement in huddles fostered unity, his voice carrying a newfound gravitas that rallied the group during slumps. Off the floor, he mentored younger players like rookie Speedy Claxton, emphasizing professionalism amid the NBA's grind. This deeper embrace of leadership wasn't performative; it stemmed from personal maturation, influenced by fatherhood and the stabilizing presence of his inner circle. Iverson's focus sharpened the team's edge, turning potential discord into synergy. As the Sixers surged, his poise under scrutiny—media still harped on his tattoos and cornrows—underscored a man redefining stardom on his terms, proving that emotional resilience could elevate a franchise. By mid-season, whispers of MVP candidacy grew louder, a testament to how Iverson's internal revolution was reshaping the narrative around him.

The Philadelphia 76ers of the 2000-01 season embodied a blue-collar ethos that mirrored the city's working-class spirit—tough, unyielding, and built on the fundamentals of defense, rebounding, and sheer physicality. This wasn't a glamour squad stacked with All-Stars; it was a gritty collective where every possession felt like a street fight, perfectly complementing Allen Iverson's explosive scoring. Under Larry Brown's system, the Sixers ranked fifth in the league in points allowed per game at 90.4, a testament to their suffocating half-court defense that forced opponents into contested shots and turnovers. Theo Ratliff, before his midseason trade to Atlanta, anchored the paint with 3.7 blocks per game, leading the NBA and instilling fear at the rim, while his replacement, Dikembe Mutombo, brought veteran presence with 2.5 blocks and 12.4 rebounds per contest after arriving in February. George Lynch and Tyrone Hill epitomized the toughness, crashing the boards with relentless energy—Hill grabbing 9.0 rebounds nightly, Lynch adding 7.2 while harassing wings with 1.2 steals. The team finished fifth in total rebounds at 44.8 per game, dominating the glass through offensive putbacks (13.1 per game) and defensive stops that transitioned into Iverson's breakneck fast breaks.

This defensive backbone amplified Iverson's offensive firepower like a well-oiled machine. While he poured in 31.1 points on acrobatic drives and pull-ups, the roster's grit ensured low-scoring affairs where his bursts could swing momentum. Eric Snow and Aaron McKie provided perimeter clamps, Snow's 1.5 steals and McKie's versatility forcing errors that Iverson converted into highlights. The synergy was evident in their 56-26 record, the best in the East, where toughness turned Iverson's individual brilliance into team dominance. Philadelphia fans revered this identity, seeing in the Sixers' scrap a reflection of their own resilience, as the team ground out wins in an era of flashier offenses. Brown's emphasis on effort over ego forged a unit where rebounding battles and defensive stands weren't just strategy—they were the heartbeat that let Iverson shine without carrying the load alone.

Amid the Sixers' defensive fortress, the most pivotal evolution occurred off the court: the once-volatile relationship between Allen Iverson and Larry Brown transforming from chaos into productive chemistry. When Brown arrived in Philadelphia in 1997, fresh off coaching stints that emphasized discipline and structure, he clashed immediately with Iverson's freewheeling style—the young guard's late nights, missed practices, and aversion to authority grated against Brown's old-school ethos. For years, their dynamic simmered with tension: public spats, trade rumors, and Brown's frustration with Iverson's individualism boiled over, nearly derailing the franchise. Iverson, in turn, viewed Brown's critiques as personal attacks, fueling a narrative of irreconcilable differences that dominated headlines.

Yet, as the 2000-01 season approached, a subtle shift emerged. Exhausted by the discord, both men sought common ground—Iverson, maturing through personal trials, began embracing Brown's system, recognizing its potential to amplify his talents. Brown, admiring Iverson's unmatched competitiveness, softened his approach, offering praise amid the pushes. This newfound synergy manifested in practices turned purposeful, where Brown's tactical drills honed Iverson's decision-making, and Iverson's intensity inspired the roster. No longer adversaries, they became collaborators: Brown designed sets to exploit Iverson's speed, while Iverson committed to defensive principles, averaging 2.5 steals per game. Teammates like Aaron McKie noted the change, describing huddles where Brown's strategies and Iverson's fire aligned seamlessly. This alchemy propelled the Sixers to dominance, turning potential implosion into the fuel for Iverson's MVP ascent. In a league of polished superstars, their reconciled partnership symbolized resilience, proving that friction, when channeled, could forge greatness. By season's midpoint, the chaos of yesteryear had yielded to a bond that Philadelphia celebrated—a coach and his star, united in pursuit of glory.

Fueled by the reconciled chemistry with Larry Brown, Allen Iverson ignited the 2000-01 season with a barrage of scoring performances that not only propelled the Sixers' historic 10-0 start but also reverberated across the NBA, signaling a shift in the Eastern Conference power dynamic. From the opening tip on October 31 at Madison Square Garden, Iverson set an aggressive tone against the Knicks, pouring in 25 points with nine assists and six rebounds in a dominant 101-72 victory, his relentless drives and perfect 13-of-14 free throws exposing New York's perimeter defense. Two nights later, hosting Toronto, he added 24 points on efficient shooting, dissecting double-teams with crossovers that left defenders grasping at air. The outbursts continued: 29 points and eight rebounds in Orlando on November 3, overwhelming the Magic in a 99-91 grind; 23 points with seven boards in Miami the next day; then 28 points against Detroit on November 8, including three timely threes that stretched the floor.

Even in lower-output games—like 18 against Minnesota or 17 versus Boston—his impact transcended the box score, with timely steals and assists fueling transitions that kept the Sixers undefeated. Averaging 23.1 points over those first 10 contests, Iverson's consistency amid high usage (often 20+ shots) showcased his endurance and adaptability, blending volume scoring with playmaking. League-wide, this hot streak forced rivals to recalibrate: coaches scrambled for schemes to slow his quickness, while analysts buzzed about Philadelphia's emergence as a title threat. Iverson's early dominance—marked by fearless penetration and clutch free-throw accuracy—ignited MVP whispers, challenging the notion that size and efficiency defined superstardom. As the wins mounted, the NBA took notice: the undersized guard from Hampton was not just surviving but dictating the pace, setting a tone of unyielding offense that would define the season's narrative and elevate the Sixers to elite status.

As Iverson's scoring rampage continued, NBA teams scrambled to devise strategies to contain the 6-foot guard whose quickness turned every matchup into a mismatch. Opponents often assigned their quickest defenders—point guards like Jason Kidd of the Suns or Mike Bibby of the Grizzlies—but Iverson's crossover dribble and explosive first step left them in his wake, forcing help that opened lanes for his teammates. In a November 11 clash with the defending champion Lakers, Derek Fisher and Kobe Bryant took turns harassing him full-court, yet Iverson dropped 35 points on 14-of-27 shooting, his relentless drives drawing fouls and frustration evident in Bryant's post-game admission of exhaustion. Double-teams became commonplace; the Knicks threw Latrell Sprewell and Allan Houston at him in waves during their opener, but Iverson's hesitation moves and step-backs neutralized the traps, leading to 25 points and a blowout win.

Taller wings like Vince Carter of the Raptors or Ray Allen of the Bucks were deployed to use length against his drives, yet Iverson exploited the speed differential, blowing by for layups or drawing charges that disrupted rhythms. In a December 23 tilt against Milwaukee, Allen's physicality—bumping defenders off-balance—yielded 46 points despite triple-teams in the fourth, underscoring the Bucks' defensive woes as they ranked top-five but couldn't stem his 18-of-18 free throws. Coaches like Doc Rivers of the Magic voiced exasperation, noting how Iverson's stamina wore down rotations, averaging 42 minutes per game while leading the league in steals at 2.5. These failures amplified league-wide panic; no scheme fully bottled his improvisational genius, turning defensive game plans into exercises in futility and fueling the MVP buzz as Iverson's dominance exposed the era's perimeter vulnerabilities.

The signature games of Allen Iverson's 2000-01 campaign were masterclasses in defiance, each outburst not just padding stats but building an unassailable MVP case through sheer willpower against elite competition. On November 12, facing the defending champion Lakers at the First Union Center, Iverson torched Kobe Bryant and company for 35 points on 14-of-27 shooting, including 6-of-7 from deep, in a gritty 98-89 victory that snapped Los Angeles' five-game win streak and announced Philadelphia as a legitimate threat. His relentless drives and step-back threes left Shaquille O'Neal and the Lakers' vaunted defense reeling, the crowd's roar echoing like a city's awakening.

Momentum surged with a December 23 showdown against the Milwaukee Bucks, where Iverson erupted for 46 points despite triple-teams, going 18-of-18 from the line in a 100-91 road win that extended the Sixers' streak and exposed the East's vulnerabilities. Then came January 6 in Cleveland, a 54-point explosion—his career high at the time—on 19-of-30 shooting, with three steals, clinching a 96-91 nail-biter against the Cavaliers and silencing doubters about his efficiency. Later, on January 21 versus Toronto, Iverson's 51 points in overtime, including acrobatic layups over Vince Carter, nearly stole a 98-96 loss, his heroics turning defeat into legend.

These statement nights—punctuated by a February 13 takedown of Milwaukee with 49 points—fueled national buzz, as Iverson's ability to will wins against contenders redefined scoring guards. Each performance layered onto the MVP narrative, showcasing not just volume but clutch dominance that propelled the Sixers to a 56-26 record, the East's top seed, and Iverson into the pantheon of undersized icons.

Beneath the highlight-reel explosions lay a grueling reality: Allen Iverson's body, at just 165 pounds, absorbed a punishing toll from his kamikaze drives and fearless forays into the paint, resulting in a litany of injuries that tested his resolve throughout the 2000-01 campaign. From early in the season, Iverson battled bursitis in his right elbow, an inflammation that swelled painfully after collisions, prompting him to adopt the black compression sleeve that became a signature part of his look—a badge of defiance rather than defeat. Hip bruises accumulated from hard falls, including a deep contusion on his left side that throbbed during games, while a bruised tailbone (sacrum contusion) from a mid-season tumble left him wincing on every cut and pivot. Sprains plagued his thumb and ankle, with a chip fracture in his right ankle lingering from prior wear, and shoulder strains flared from defensive hacks. Despite these ailments, Iverson missed only 11 games, averaging a league-high 42 minutes per night, his wiry frame logging more court time than any player as he led the NBA in scoring and steals.

This "play through everything" mentality defined Iverson, a ethos forged in Hampton's streets where quitting wasn't an option. Teammates marveled at his refusal to sit; as Aaron McKie noted, Iverson would tape up, grit his teeth, and perform, often dropping 30-plus points amid visible limps. In an era before load management, he embodied unyielding toughness, once quipping he'd "rest during practice" rather than miss battles. The physical toll was evident—bruises mottling his arms, ice packs post-game—but it amplified his legend, proving an undersized guard could dominate through sheer will. Philadelphia fans, accustomed to hard knocks, idolized this resilience, seeing in Iverson's pain-fueled heroics a mirror of their own perseverance. As the MVP chatter intensified, his ability to thrive despite the battering reshaped perceptions of durability, turning personal sacrifice into the cornerstone of the Sixers' improbable rise.

In the heart of Philadelphia, a city forged in the fires of revolution and resilient blue-collar pride, Allen Iverson wasn't just a basketball player—he was a living emblem of its unpolished soul, igniting an emotional bond that crackled with electricity through the 2000-01 season. Fans, weary from decades of mediocrity since the 1983 title, saw in Iverson a reflection of their own struggles: the undersized fighter from humble beginnings, tattooed and cornrowed, who defied the odds with raw authenticity. As the Sixers surged, arenas pulsed with chants of "A.I.! A.I.!"—a rhythmic heartbeat echoing through South Philly streets, where murals of his crossover began appearing on brick walls. This connection ran deeper than wins; it was cultural alchemy, Iverson's hip-hop-infused swagger—Reebok sneakers, baggy shorts, and unapologetic vibe—resonating with a diverse fanbase, from inner-city youth to suburban diehards, who embraced him as a symbol of rebellion against the NBA's polished elite.

Emotionally, the tie was profound; Iverson's "play through pain" ethos mirrored Philly's ethos of endurance, turning his bruises into shared scars. When he dropped 46 on Milwaukee or battled Shaq in the spotlight, fans felt the hits, their roars a collective exhale of pent-up frustration. Yet, this love was electric and complicated—Philly's rabid supporters could turn critical, as Iverson later recalled the "wrath" of their expectations, but it fueled him, transforming boos into motivation. Culturally, he reshaped youth aspirations, inspiring a generation to embrace individuality amid a conformist league. By season's end, the bond had electrified the city, packing the First Union Center with unprecedented energy, as Iverson's MVP chase became a communal triumph, proving that in Philadelphia, stardom wasn't gifted—it was earned through grit and heart.

As the MVP momentum built through the winter of 2001, Allen Iverson's influence transcended basketball courts, permeating fashion, swagger, and youth culture with an unapologetic authenticity that challenged the NBA's buttoned-up image. His cornrows, intricate tattoos, and baggy jerseys—often paired with diamond chains and oversized Reebok sneakers—became blueprints for streetwear, inspiring a generation of young fans to embrace hip-hop aesthetics over traditional athletic polish. Iverson's arm sleeve, initially a practical cover for his elbow injury, evolved into a style staple, symbolizing resilience and flair, as kids across urban America replicated his look, blending sport and street culture in malls and playgrounds. This wasn't mere imitation; it was empowerment, as Iverson's swagger—cocky crossovers, trash-talking bravado, and fearless drives—embodied a defiant attitude that rejected conformity, urging youth to own their identities amid societal scrutiny.

At the height of his push, Iverson fused Black culture with the league's mainstream, introducing elements like durags and throwback jerseys that sparked debates but ultimately normalized diversity. His attitude, raw and unfiltered, resonated with disenfranchised teens, who saw in him a hero who rose from poverty without compromising his roots, influencing music videos, rap lyrics, and schoolyard ball where "A.I. moves" became synonymous with individuality. Philadelphia amplified this cultural wave, with local artists and fans adopting his vibe, turning the city into a hub of edgy expression. Yet, this impact drew backlash from conservative corners, highlighting tensions around race and representation. As MVP votes loomed, Iverson's off-court revolution proved as potent as his on-court dominance, redefining cool for a new era and leaving an indelible mark on how athletes expressed themselves.

Even as Allen Iverson's on-court heroics captivated fans and reshaped youth culture, a chorus of media commentators and league gatekeepers persisted in questioning his suitability as the face of a franchise, scrutinizing his style, leadership, and off-court persona with a skepticism that often veered into cultural bias. NBA Commissioner David Stern, the ultimate arbiter of the league's image, viewed Iverson's hip-hop affiliations and unfiltered demeanor as threats to the NBA's marketability, reportedly summoning him for a stern lecture over the controversial lyrics in his unreleased rap album "Non-Fiction," which included homophobic slurs and violent imagery that drew widespread condemnation in October 2000. Stern's discomfort symbolized broader institutional unease, as Iverson's cornrows, tattoos, and entourage clashed with the polished professionalism the league promoted.

Columnists amplified the doubts: Phil Mushnick of the New York Post relentlessly portrayed Iverson as a symbol of the NBA's moral decline, lambasting his "thug" image and leadership style as divisive, even as the Sixers dominated the East. ESPN's Dan Patrick drew parallels to baseball's John Rocker, criticizing the rap single "40 Bars" for its offensive content toward gays and women, questioning whether Iverson's authenticity masked irresponsibility. Sports Illustrated's Jack McCallum, in a pointed piece, highlighted the disconnect between Iverson's lavish lifestyle and the "ugly worldview" in his music, fueling debates on whether his swagger undermined team cohesion. These critiques, often laced with racial undertones—Iverson was deemed "too Black, too 'hood"—persisted despite his MVP-caliber play, reflecting a media landscape resistant to his redefinition of stardom. Yet, this opposition only heightened the drama, casting Iverson as a rebel icon whose resilience against the establishment mirrored his on-court battles.

Allen Iverson's 2001 MVP award wasn't just a personal triumph; it shattered the NBA's entrenched expectations of what an MVP should embody, compelling the league to confront and redefine notions of greatness in an era dominated by towering, polished archetypes. Traditionally, MVPs like Michael Jordan or Shaquille O'Neal exemplified size, efficiency, and market-friendly personas—tall, dominant figures with clean-cut images that aligned with corporate endorsements. At a mere 6 feet and 165 pounds, Iverson defied the physical blueprint, becoming the shortest MVP since the 1950s and the first guard to win since Magic Johnson in 1990, leading the league in scoring (31.1 points) and steals (2.5) while dragging a gritty Sixers squad to 56 wins. His style further upended norms: cornrows, full-sleeve tattoos, and hip-hop flair—baggy jeans, chains, and a compression sleeve born from injury—challenged the league's conservative aesthetics, blending street culture with professional sports in ways that drew ire from purists but resonated with a new demographic.

Iverson's background amplified the revolution—from a poverty-stricken upbringing in Hampton, Virginia, marked by legal troubles including a controversial jail stint, to rising as an unapologetic icon who embraced rap and urban swagger. This narrative forced reevaluation: greatness wasn't confined to height or homogeneity but could thrive through relentlessness, cultural authenticity, and individual brilliance. As Commissioner Stern grappled with Iverson's influence, the award symbolized a pivot, paving the way for future undersized stars like Stephen Curry and culturally bold athletes who prioritized self-expression. Iverson didn't fit the mold—he demolished it, proving that in the NBA's evolving landscape, heart and hustle could eclipse convention.

As the 2000-01 season barreled toward its climax, Allen Iverson transcended his role as the Sixers' scoring savant, emerging as an unavoidable epicenter of NBA coverage, cultural debates, and sports media scrutiny that redefined the league's narrative. National outlets like ESPN and Sports Illustrated dissected his every move, from 50-point outbursts to off-court antics, framing him as the anti-hero in a sport grappling with its identity. The controversy surrounding his unreleased rap album, initially titled "Non-Fiction" and featuring the single "40 Bars," erupted in October 2000, igniting fierce debates over lyrics laden with homophobic slurs, misogyny, and violent imagery. Commissioner David Stern publicly condemned the content as "coarse, offensive, and anti-social," summoning Iverson for a meeting that underscored the tension between street culture and corporate basketball.

Media pundits piled on: ABC News reported on calls for fines or suspensions, while advocacy groups demanded accountability, turning Iverson into a flashpoint for discussions on race, representation, and athlete responsibility. Iverson's eventual apology to gays and women in early October did little to quell the storm, as columnists debated whether his "thug" persona—cornrows, tattoos, and hip-hop ties—threatened the NBA's family-friendly image. Yet, this media maelstrom amplified his stardom; ratings soared for Sixers games, and cultural commentators hailed him as a bridge between urban authenticity and mainstream sports. By mid-season, Iverson wasn't just covered—he was the conversation, forcing the league to confront its biases while his on-court brilliance demanded respect amid the noise.

On May 15, 2001, in a ceremony at the First Union Center before Game 2 of the Eastern Conference Semifinals against Toronto, Allen Iverson stepped onto the court to accept the NBA MVP trophy from Commissioner David Stern, becoming the first Philadelphia 76er to claim the honor since Moses Malone in 1983. Garnering 93 of 124 first-place votes and appearing on every ballot, Iverson edged out Shaquille O'Neal and Tim Duncan, his 31.1 points, 4.6 assists, and 2.5 steals per game underscoring a season of unrelenting dominance. At 6 feet tall—the shortest MVP in league history since the award's inception in 1956—this victory symbolized the triumph of the underdog, a wiry guard from Hampton's projects who outwilled giants through speed, heart, and improvisation, challenging the NBA's bias toward size and structure.

Culturally, Iverson's win was a seismic shift, affirming Black street culture's place in the mainstream NBA—a league once resistant to cornrows, tattoos, and hip-hop swagger. It represented authenticity over assimilation, inspiring marginalized youth to see themselves in stardom without compromise, as Iverson's journey from incarceration to icon dismantled barriers of race and class. Emotionally, the moment electrified Philadelphia, fans erupting in ovations that echoed the city's blue-collar pride, tears streaming as Iverson, voice cracking, thanked his supporters amid the roar. For Iverson, it was vindication after years of doubt, a raw outpouring of gratitude that humanized his defiance. As confetti fell, the MVP mantle not only crowned his season but propelled the Sixers into the playoffs with unbreakable momentum, ready to etch their grit into postseason lore.

With the MVP trophy in hand, Allen Iverson and the Philadelphia 76ers stood on the precipice of immortality, their 56-26 regular-season record securing the top seed in the Eastern Conference and igniting a city long dormant in championship dreams. The campaign had been a symphony of grit: Iverson's league-leading 31.1 points and 2.5 steals per game, amplified by Dikembe Mutombo's rim protection after the February trade, and a defense that surrendered just 90.4 points nightly, fifth-best in the NBA. Larry Brown's squad, once fractured, now pulsed with unity—role players like Aaron McKie and Eric Snow embodying the blue-collar ethos that mirrored Philly's streets. Iverson's evolution from rebel to redeemer had not only silenced critics but galvanized a fanbase, his cultural imprint—swagger, style, and unyielding heart—fusing with the team's identity to create something transcendent.

As April wound down, anticipation built like storm clouds over the Benjamin Franklin Bridge. The First Union Center thrummed with sold-out crowds, murals of Iverson's crossover adorning South Philly walls, and local radio buzzing about a potential Finals clash with the defending champion Lakers. Iverson, battered but unbreakable, embodied the city's resilient spirit, his MVP win a beacon for underdogs everywhere. Whispers of destiny filled locker rooms; Brown drilled fundamentals with playoff intensity, while Iverson's quiet confidence infected the roster. Philadelphia, starved for glory since 1983, sensed history in the making—a scrappy collective poised to challenge the league's giants. As the regular season faded, the Sixers stepped into the 2001 playoffs, ready to unleash their fury on an unsuspecting postseason.

The 2001 Finals

The Philadelphia 76ers staggered into the 2001 NBA Finals like warriors fresh from a battlefield, their bodies battered and spirits tested by a postseason odyssey that had pushed them to the brink. After dispatching the Indiana Pacers in a relatively swift 3-1 first-round series, the real crucible began. Against Vince Carter and the Toronto Raptors in the Eastern Conference Semifinals, the Sixers endured a seven-game war, trading blows in a series defined by clutch performances and heartbreaking near-misses. Iverson, already nursing injuries from the regular season, poured in averages of over 30 points per game, his wiry frame absorbing contact that would sideline lesser players.

Barely catching their breath, they faced Ray Allen and the Milwaukee Bucks in the Conference Finals—another grueling seven-game slog. Game 7 in Philadelphia's First Union Center was a microcosm of their resilience: a 108-91 victory sealed amid roaring crowds, but at a cost. Players like Eric Snow and Aaron McKie played through sprains and strains, while Dikembe Mutombo anchored the defense with bruised ribs. The toll was visible—dark circles under eyes, limps in strides, ice packs a constant companion. The Lakers, meanwhile, had cruised through the West with three consecutive sweeps, entering the Finals rested and regal.

Yet, as the team plane touched down in Los Angeles, defiance burned brighter than fatigue. This wasn't just about basketball; it was a cultural standoff. Iverson, the undersized icon from Hampton, Virginia, embodied Philly's blue-collar grit against the Hollywood glamour of Shaq and Kobe. The emotional stakes loomed large: for a franchise starved of success since 1983, this was redemption. For Black America and hip-hop enthusiasts, Iverson's journey—from poverty and legal troubles to MVP status—represented unyielding rebellion. The Sixers arrived exhausted, yes, but with a fire that whispered of miracles. In the shadow of the Staples Center, they stood ready to defy the odds, knowing every ache carried the weight of a city's dreams and a culture's defiance.

The Los Angeles Lakers loomed over the 2001 NBA Finals like a colossus, their dominance an unyielding force that had reshaped the league's landscape. As defending champions, they entered the series with an aura of inevitability, a blend of Hollywood glamour and ruthless efficiency that intimidated opponents before tip-off. Under coach Phil Jackson's Zen mastery, the team had swept through the Western Conference playoffs untouched—dispatching Portland in three, Sacramento in four, and San Antonio in another four—extending a postseason winning streak to 15 games. Their record screamed supremacy: 56-26 in the regular season, but it was the playoffs where they transformed into something mythic.

At the heart of this juggernaut pulsed the Shaq-Kobe tandem, a devastating synergy of power and finesse. Shaquille O'Neal, the 7-foot-1 behemoth, averaged 27 points and 13 rebounds in the playoffs, his sheer mass crumpling defenses like paper. Kobe Bryant, emerging from Shaq's shadow, added 29 points per game with acrobatic grace, their partnership a volatile alchemy of ego and excellence that fueled whispers of dynasty. The Lakers' bench—Robert

Horry's clutch shots, Derek Fisher's steady hand—amplified the threat, creating an ensemble cast backed by Tinseltown's spotlight.

For Philadelphia, this was an impossible mountain, a David versus Goliath scripted for heartbreak. The Sixers, weary from their Eastern battles, faced a rested powerhouse favored by double digits. Iverson's speed clashed against Shaq's immovable object, Mutombo's finger-wag paling before the Diesel's roar. Culturally, it pitted street-ball rebellion against corporate polish, Philly's grit against L.A.'s gloss. The odds screamed futility, yet in that disparity lay the emotional charge—a underdog's prayer against an empire's decree.

The 2001 NBA Finals transcended basketball, erupting into a cultural flashpoint that pitted Allen Iverson's raw rebellion against the Los Angeles Lakers' polished dynasty machine. Iverson, with his cornrows, tattoos, and unapologetic street ethos, became a lightning rod for a shifting America. He represented the underdog's fury—Black America, hip-hop heads, and disaffected youth who saw in his crossover dribble a defiance of the establishment. The NBA, still grappling with its image post-Jordan, viewed Iverson as a disruptor: too brash, too urban, his baggy shorts and arm sleeves symbols of a culture clash. Against him stood the Lakers, a well-oiled empire embodying corporate excellence—Shaq's dominant force paired with Kobe's surgical precision, all under Phil Jackson's serene command. They were the favorites, the inevitability, Hollywood's scripted victors.

As the series unfolded, national storylines amplified the drama. Media dissected Iverson's journey from Hampton's hardships to MVP glory, framing it as a battle for the soul of the sport. Hip-hop artists like Jay-Z and DMX rallied behind him, his style influencing fashion and attitude league-wide. The Finals spotlighted racial undertones: Iverson's grit resonated with communities weary of conformity, while the Lakers symbolized the league's push for mainstream appeal. Even in defeat, Iverson's stand sparked conversations on authenticity versus assimilation, rebellion versus regime.

This matchup wasn't just games; it was a manifesto. Iverson's isolation plays mirrored freestyle battles, his resilience echoing hip-hop's hustle narrative. The Lakers' machine rolled on, but Iverson's fire ignited a cultural shift, proving grit could challenge giants and redefine heroism in sports.

As the lights dimmed in Staples Center on June 6, 2001, Allen Iverson stepped onto the court with a mindset forged in fire—defiant, unyielding, a street-fighter's glare masking the exhaustion from Philly's playoff marathon. The MVP knew the narrative: his Sixers were sacrificial lambs to the Lakers' dynasty, outmatched in size, depth, and rest. But Iverson's psyche thrived on doubt; it was fuel for his crossover dreams, a rebellion against the league's polished facade. Tattoos peeking from his sleeves, cornrows tight, he embodied the underdog's rage, whispering to himself that this was his moment to silence the skeptics who questioned his size, his style, his survival.

The energy in the building crackled like static electricity, a mix of Hollywood entitlement and uneasy anticipation. Purple and gold banners swayed above courtside celebrities—Jack Nicholson smirking, Denzel Washington nodding—while Lakers fans roared with championship arrogance, expecting a coronation. Yet an undercurrent of tension hummed; whispers of Iverson's MVP season and Philly's grit pierced the complacency. The air was thick with cultural stakes—hip-hop beats pulsing through warm-ups, symbolizing a clash of worlds: urban hustle versus Tinseltown gloss.

From tip-off, the pace exploded in a frenzy, Iverson dictating tempo like a maestro of chaos. He darted through screens, his quickness a blur against Kobe's defense, pushing the ball in transition to exploit L.A.'s lumbering frontcourt. Early buckets rained—threes from Snow, Mutombo's blocks echoing— as the Sixers jumped to a 16-5 lead, stunning the crowd into murmurs. Iverson's drives sliced like knives, drawing fouls and free throws, his intensity infectious, turning fatigue into fury. The game pulsed with raw emotion, each possession a micro-battle in a war where heart challenged hardware, setting the stage for an upset that would echo through basketball lore.

As the game intensified in the second quarter of Game 1, Allen Iverson ignited a scoring rampage that transformed Staples Center into his personal arena of defiance. With the Sixers trailing early, Iverson shifted gears, his crossover dribbles blurring past Kobe Bryant and Derek Fisher, sinking mid-range jumpers and drawing fouls with relentless drives. By halftime, he had already tallied 20 points, his wiry frame absorbing contact while keeping Philadelphia within striking distance, the score knotted at 56-56. The crowd, once buoyant with Lakers loyalty, fell into uneasy murmurs as Iverson's intensity exposed cracks in the champions' armor.

In the third quarter, the rampage escalated—Iverson poured in 16 more points, mixing step-back threes with acrobatic layups, his 3-of-8 from beyond the arc a testament to fearless shot-making. He orchestrated pick-and-rolls with precision, dishing assists to Aaron McKie and Tyrone Hill when double-teams swarmed, but it was his scoring that single-handedly sustained the Sixers. As the Lakers mounted runs, fueled by Shaq's dominance inside, Iverson answered every bucket, his 18-of-41 field goals a volume shooter's symphony, converting 9-of-9 free throws to maintain the pulse. By regulation's end, his 41 points had forced overtime, the Sixers alive solely through his will.

In the extra period, Iverson sealed his masterpiece with seven more points, including clutch free throws and a dagger three, finishing with 48 points, six assists, five rebounds, and five steals in 52 grueling minutes. His performance wasn't just stats; it was emotional alchemy, turning fatigue into ferocity, keeping a depleted team breathing against an empire. Culturally, it resonated as a Black underdog's stand, hip-hop's rhythm in motion, proving one man's grit could defy destiny, even if just for one night.

In the waning seconds of overtime in Game 1, with the Sixers clinging to a two-point lead and the Staples Center crowd on edge, Allen Iverson isolated on the right baseline against Tyronn Lue, the Lakers' scrappy defender tasked with shadowing him. The air crackled with tension, Iverson's eyes locked in predatory focus, embodying the underdog's fury against a dynasty's disdain. He jabbed right, feinting a drive, then unleashed his signature crossover—a lightning-quick dribble between his legs that snapped Lue's ankles, sending the guard stumbling as he twisted to contest.

Iverson elevated smoothly, his wiry frame hanging in the air for a split second, releasing a pristine 16-foot fadeaway jumper over Lue's outstretched hand. The ball arced perfectly, swishing through the net to push the lead to four, silencing the Hollywood faithful and igniting a roar from Philly partisans watching nationwide. Lue, sprawled on the hardwood after tripping over Iverson's leg in the contest, looked up in defeat as the MVP paused deliberately, planting one foot over his fallen foe in a bold, unapologetic stepover—a gesture dripping with street-ball swagger and cultural defiance.

That image—frozen in time, Iverson glaring down before trotting away—became one of sports history's most iconic, symbolizing rebellion against the establishment. For Black America and hip-hop culture, it was a mic-drop moment, Iverson's grit personified, transcending the 107-101 upset to etch his legend as the fearless warrior who dared to dominate the giants, even if the series would slip away.

The stepover moment detonated like a cultural bomb, rippling through America's veins in real time, transforming a single play into a symbol of unbridled rebellion. On TV, ESPN's SportsCenter looped the highlight endlessly that night, anchors dissecting Iverson's glare and stride as a defiant punctuation to his 48-point opus, framing it as the underdog's roar against the Lakers' empire. Networks like NBC, broadcasting the Finals, replayed it in slow motion during postgame analysis, sparking debates on sportsmanship—some called it trashy, others triumphant—while viewership spiked, drawing in non-basketball fans captivated by the drama.

Radio waves crackled with immediate fervor; sports talk shows from Philly's WIP to L.A.'s AM stations buzzed with callers, Black hosts hailing it as empowerment, white pundits decrying the "thug" image, amplifying Iverson's polarizing persona. In barbershops across urban America, particularly in Black communities, the scene ignited passionate discussions—clippers pausing mid-cut as patrons reenacted the step, seeing it as a victory for street culture over corporate polish, a nod to resilience amid systemic doubt.

Hip-hop spaces erupted in solidarity; DJs on Hot 97 and Power 106 spun tracks nodding to Iverson's swagger, artists like DMX and Jay-Z referencing his ethos in cyphers and lyrics, the moment cementing AI as rap's basketball avatar. Even the nascent internet—message boards on InsideHoops and RealGM, AOL chat rooms—lit up instantly, grainy GIFs circulating like wildfire, memes birthing before the term existed, fueling online wars between East Coast grit and West Coast glamour. Nationally, it stirred emotional currents in Black America, youth embracing Iverson's authenticity as a blueprint for defiance, turning a Finals footnote into a lasting emblem of cultural shift, where one step bridged sport, race, and resistance.

After the stunning overtime loss in Game 1, where Allen Iverson's 48-point eruption exposed vulnerabilities in their vaunted defense, the Los Angeles Lakers transformed into a merciless machine, their adjustments a masterclass in championship recalibration under Phil Jackson's steady hand. Shaquille O'Neal, stung by the defeat and motivated by Jackson's call for defensive aggression, unleashed his full dominance inside, averaging 33 points and 15.8 rebounds across the series while swatting 3.4 blocks per game, his sheer force crumpling

Philadelphia's interior like a tin can. In Game 2, O'Neal nearly notched a quadruple-double with 28 points, 20 rebounds, nine assists, and eight blocks, exploiting double-teams by dishing to open shooters, turning the paint into his personal fiefdom as the Lakers rolled to a 98-89 victory.

Kobe Bryant, emerging from the shadows of Game 1's inefficiency, locked in with assertive scoring and playmaking, posting 24.6 points, 7.8 rebounds, and 5.8 assists per game. His 31-point outburst in Game 2, coupled with eight rebounds and six assists, signaled the shift—Bryant attacked mismatches in the triangle offense, driving and kicking to dismantle the Sixers' schemes. Defensively, the Lakers clamped down on Iverson; Derek Fisher took primary duties, denying drives and forcing perimeter shots, limiting the MVP to inefficient outings like 10-of-29 in Game 2, while Tyronn Lue provided pesky relief. Fastbreak points surged (25-9 edge in Game 2), capitalizing on forced turnovers as L.A. slowed the pace, leveraging their size and rest advantage.

The dominance unfolded relentlessly: a gritty 96-91 win in Game 3, fueled by Bryant's 32 points and clutch plays; a 100-86 rout in Game 4 with O'Neal's 34 points; and a 108-96 closeout in Game 5, where Shaq's 29 points sealed the 4-1 series triumph. Emotionally, it was a cultural assertion—Hollywood's empire reasserting order over Philly's rebellion, Shaq and Kobe's synergy a thunderous reminder of dynasty might, leaving Iverson's fire dimmed but his legend intact.

Even as the Los Angeles Lakers tightened their grip after Game 1, the Philadelphia 76ers embodied the unyielding spirit of their city, fighting with a ferocity that turned inevitable defeat into a badge of honor. Outmatched in size, depth, and freshness, the Sixers refused to fold, channeling Philadelphia's blue-collar ethos—tough, resilient, and defiant in the face of adversity. In Game 2, despite a 98-89 loss, they clawed back from double-digit deficits, Iverson dropping 23 points on weary legs while Mutombo hauled in 22 rebounds, his finger-wags a symbol of resistance against Shaq's onslaught. The crowd at Staples sensed it: this wasn't a rout; it was a battle.

Back home in Game 3, the First Union Center erupted as the Sixers pushed the Lakers to the brink in a 96-91 heartbreaker. Iverson poured in 35 points, his drives a whirlwind of emotion, while the team forced 14 turnovers, their hustle mirroring Philly's working-class grind—scraping for every loose ball, every stop, as if the city's soul depended on it. Even in the blowouts of Games 4 (100-86) and 5 (108-96), Philadelphia's fight shone through: a 51-rebound effort in the finale, Snow's gritty defense, McKie's timely threes. Culturally, it resonated—Black fans and hip-hop communities saw Iverson's battered body as a metaphor for systemic struggles, his refusal to quit inspiring youth to embrace authenticity over surrender.

This mismatch wasn't just athletic; it was philosophical, Philly's underdog heart against L.A.'s machine. The Sixers' persistence, averaging 93.8 points while holding the Lakers under 101 in three games, captured the essence of a city built on comebacks, turning loss into a cultural victory that deepened Iverson's legend. The 2001 NBA Finals ignited a firestorm of conversations that probed the league's soul, unraveling threads of image, toughness, authenticity, and hip-hop culture in ways that reverberated far beyond the court. Allen Iverson, with his cornrows, tattoos, and oversized jerseys, shattered the NBA's post-Jordan facade of polished professionalism—a clean-cut, corporate-friendly image championed by Commissioner David Stern. Pundits debated whether Iverson's urban aesthetic threatened the league's marketability, sparking national discourse on racial biases and the commodification of Black athletes, as media outlets like Sports Illustrated dissected his "thug" label versus his unfiltered realness.

Toughness emerged as a central theme, Iverson's 6-foot frame enduring brutal physicality—averaging 52 minutes in the series despite injuries—redefining resilience in a sport dominated by giants. His refusal to back down against Shaq's might symbolized inner-city grit, challenging notions of manhood and perseverance that resonated in barbershops and locker rooms alike.

Authenticity pulsed at the heart of it all; Iverson's journey from poverty and incarceration to MVP stardom embodied raw truth, contrasting the manufactured personas of many stars. This authenticity dovetailed with hip-hop culture, where Iverson's crossover dribbles mirrored freestyle battles, his style influencing artists like Jadakiss and fueling NBA-rap crossovers. Youth and Black America embraced him as a beacon, sparking debates on cultural appropriation versus celebration within the league. The Finals didn't just crown the Lakers; they forced the NBA to confront its evolving identity, paving the way for a more inclusive, expressive era where toughness and hip-hop became integral to the game's fabric.

As the series shifted after Game 1, the Los Angeles Lakers' depth and power asserted an inexorable dominance, their roster a well-tuned engine that overwhelmed Philadelphia's valiant but limited resistance. Shaquille O'Neal, the Finals MVP, bulldozed through the paint with 33 points and 15.8 rebounds per game, his sheer physicality rendering Dikembe Mutombo's blocks mere gestures, while Kobe Bryant complemented with 24.6 points, 7.8 rebounds, and 5.8 assists, his versatility slicing through defenses. But it was the supporting cast that sealed the takeover—Derek Fisher draining threes at 52.6% for 9.8 points, Rick Fox adding 9.8 points and defensive grit, Robert Horry contributing 8.4 points and timely blocks, their collective contributions exposing the Sixers' lack of bench firepower. The Lakers won the next four games by an average of 8 points, their triangle offense flowing seamlessly, turning mismatches into routs as Philadelphia's fatigue mounted.

Yet Allen Iverson's indomitable presence refused to let the series devolve into failure, his 35.6 points per game on 47.4 minutes a heroic stand that infused every contest with emotional gravity. Battered and bloodied, Iverson shouldered the offense, his drives and step-backs a defiant poetry against inevitable defeat, averaging 5.6 rebounds and 3.8 assists amid swarming defenses. For youth, hip-hop fans, and Black America, his unyielding fight symbolized authenticity over surrender, turning a 4-1 loss into a cultural triumph. The Finals weren't a rout; they were a testament to one man's will, deepening Iverson's legend as the rebel who made giants sweat.

As the final buzzer sounded in Game 5 of the 2001 NBA Finals, with the Los Angeles Lakers claiming a 108-96 victory and their second straight championship, Allen Iverson stood amid the confetti-strewn court, his body broken but his aura unbreakable. The Sixers had fallen 4-1, outgunned by Shaq's dominance and Kobe's precision, yet defeat did not diminish Iverson—it catapulted him into immortality. Averaging 35.6 points, 5.6 rebounds, and 3.8 assists over the series, while logging a grueling 47.4 minutes per game, Iverson's herculean efforts painted him as the ultimate warrior, a 6-foot David who made Goliaths bleed. His 48-point masterpiece in Game 1, capped by the stepover, lingered as a cultural totem, but even in losses—like his 37 points in the finale amid swelling ankles and exhaustion—his refusal to yield deepened the legend.

Nationally, the narrative shifted: Iverson wasn't a loser; he was a rebel icon whose authenticity triumphed over rings. For Black America, his cornrowed defiance against the league's establishment echoed broader struggles, inspiring youth to embrace unfiltered self-expression. Hip-hop embraced him tighter—artists sampling his ethos in lyrics, fans in barbershops debating his toughness as the essence of real. The Finals loss became a pyrrhic victory, proving Iverson's impact transcended trophies; it reshaped NBA culture, ushering in an era where individuality rivaled championships. In defeat, Iverson's legend swelled, 2001 etching itself as the pinnacle of the AI era—a moment where heart outshone hardware, forever altering how greatness is measured.

The 2001 NBA Finals etched itself as a defining chapter in league history, a cinematic clash where underdog rebellion collided with dynasty might, forever altering the narrative of what constitutes greatness in basketball. Amid a post-Jordan era hungry for icons, Allen Iverson's Sixers challenging the Shaq-Kobe Lakers became a cultural referendum on style, substance, and soul—Philly's gritty authenticity versus L.A.'s polished dominance. The series, though a 4-1 Lakers victory, is immortalized for Game 1's upset and Iverson's 48-point opus, culminating in the stepover on Tyronn Lue, a moment that symbolized unapologetic swagger and resonated as one of the NBA's top Finals highlights. Iverson's herculean averages—35.6 points over grueling minutes—proved a small guard could drag a team to the brink, inspiring debates on whether rings define legacy or if heart and hustle do.

For Iverson, the Finals amplified his mythos as the NBA's ultimate disruptor, a modern-day Muhammad Ali in cornrows, polarizing yet profoundly honest, forcing white America to confront aspects of Black culture through his hip-hop-infused persona. His unstoppable play, as recalled by opponents like Horace Grant, underscored a deserved MVP season, blending street-ball flair with relentless toughness that inspired generations to embrace authenticity and never yield. Though ringless, Iverson's 2001 run—capped by four scoring titles and cultural shifts in fashion and attitude—cemented him as a legend whose influence transcended wins, redefining heroism in sports. This era-defining moment marked the pinnacle of the AI Era, where one man's defiance reshaped the game's very ethos, proving that sometimes, the fight itself forges immortality.

The 2001 NBA Finals stand as the indelible apex of Allen Iverson's legend, a seismic moment where his unyielding spirit collided with destiny, forever etching the AI Era into the annals of sports and culture. In those five games, Iverson didn't just play basketball; he waged a visceral rebellion, his 35.6 points per contest a manifesto of defiance that transcended the scoreboard. Though the Sixers fell 4-1 to the Lakers' juggernaut, Iverson's masterpiece—capped by the stepover on Tyronn Lue—became a cultural talisman, symbolizing authenticity in a world demanding conformity. For Black America, it was empowerment personified, a tattooed underdog from Hampton's streets proving that grit could challenge empires, inspiring generations to embrace their roots amid systemic pressures.

Decades later, the ripples endure. Iverson's influence permeates the NBA, where cornrows and arm sleeves are no longer outliers but emblems of self-expression, hip-hop's rhythm woven into the game's fabric. Youth in urban courts mimic his crossover, barbershop debates echo his toughness, and artists from Kendrick Lamar to Lil Wayne nod to his ethos in lyrics that celebrate rebellion. The Finals sparked dialogues on race, image, and resilience that reshaped league policies and fan perceptions, paving the way for stars like Russell Westbrook and Kyrie Irving to thrive unapologetically. Even without a ring, 2001 elevated Iverson to mythic status—a defining chapter where one man's fire ignited a cultural revolution, reminding the world that legends aren't forged in victory alone, but in the unquenchable will to fight.

The Style Revolution

When Allen Iverson burst onto the NBA scene in 1996, selected first overall by the Philadelphia 76ers, he arrived not just as a player but as a cultural detonator, his visual identity a stark departure from the league's polished, corporate veneer. At 6 feet tall and 165 pounds, Iverson's wiry frame was clad in oversized jerseys that draped like urban capes, baggy shorts sagging with street authenticity, and an arm sleeve that would become his signature armor. His cornrows, intricately braided and often topped with a headband, evoked the rhythmic flows of hip-hop artists like Tupac and Biggie, whose influence pulsed through his veins from Hampton, Virginia's tough neighborhoods. Tattoos peeked from beneath his uniform, inked stories of survival and rebellion that contrasted sharply with the clean-cut images of predecessors like Michael Jordan or Magic Johnson, who embodied the NBA's mainstream appeal.

This raw expressiveness rooted in hip-hop aesthetics—flashy chains glinting under arena lights, do-rags during warm-ups—challenged the establishment's expectations, injecting the league with an unfiltered Black urban ethos that had simmered on playgrounds but rarely graced national stages. Iverson's style wasn't performative; it was lived, a mirror to the hip-hop explosion of the late '90s, where artists like Jay-Z and DMX championed unapologetic selfhood amid societal scrutiny. Younger fans, particularly in Black communities, saw themselves reflected in his defiance, a visual manifesto that blended vulnerability with unbreakable toughness. Socially, it sparked unease among league officials, who viewed his look as a threat to marketability, yet historically, it marked a turning point, grounding the NBA in the cultural shifts of a generation demanding authenticity over assimilation. Iverson didn't just play the game; he visually redefined it, his emergence a bold declaration that hip-hop's heartbeat could echo through professional sports.

Allen Iverson's cornrows emerged as an instant emblem of cultural identity, pride, and resistance upon his NBA debut, transcending mere hairstyle to become a bold declaration of unapologetic Blackness in a league long dominated by assimilationist norms. Rooted in African traditions where braids served as maps of escape during slavery and symbols of communal heritage, Iverson's intricate rows—kept fresh and often adorned—echoed the resilience of Black communities, channeling the spirit of hip-hop pioneers who reclaimed aesthetics as acts of defiance. In the late '90s, as hip-hop surged into mainstream consciousness, Iverson's braids challenged the NBA's clean-cut archetype, embodied by figures like Michael Jordan, forcing a confrontation with racial biases and the commodification of Black athletes.

Media often coded criticism as concerns over "professionalism," but for younger fans, especially in urban Black spaces, his look mirrored their realities—pride in cultural roots amid societal scrutiny. Historically grounded in post-Civil Rights movements toward self-expression, Iverson's cornrows resisted the league's efforts to dictate basketball culture, inspiring a generation to wear their heritage visibly and unyieldingly. Not a fleeting trend, they represented resistance against erasure, blending vulnerability from his Hampton upbringing with the toughness of street survival, making Iverson a cultural lodestar who normalized Black pride on global courts. This statement hairstyle didn't just adorn his head; it crowned a revolution, proving that identity could be both armor and art in the face of institutional discomfort.

Allen Iverson's tattoos transformed his body into a living canvas of personal history, raw emotion, and unyielding defiance, challenging an NBA landscape that long favored invisible ink beneath starched uniforms. Emerging in the late '90s, his over 30 tattoos—visible during drives and dunks—narrated a life forged in Hampton's unforgiving streets: the Chinese character for "loyalty" etched on his neck, a testament to unbreakable bonds with family and crew amid betrayal and loss. "Only the Strong Survive," scripted across his abdomen with a bulldog snarling beneath, encapsulated the emotional toll of his mother's struggles, his own incarceration, and the grit required to rise from poverty, blending vulnerability with the fierce pride of Black resilience. Dedications like "Cru Thik" for his childhood posse and names of loved ones inked on his arms evoked communal ties, turning skin into a shrine of remembrance and motivation.

In a league still echoing Michael Jordan's clean-cut era, where visible tattoos were subtly discouraged as unprofessional—coded language often laced with racial undertones—Iverson's ink stood as rebellion. Rooted in hip-hop's tradition of bodily storytelling, akin to artists like Tupac whose tattoos chronicled pain and power, Iverson's defied the NBA's assimilationist pressures, asserting authenticity over marketability. Socially, it resonated in Black communities as a badge of survival, inspiring youth to wear their histories proudly, while provoking media discomfort that highlighted deeper cultural divides. His tattoos weren't adornments; they were emotional armor, historical markers, and defiant declarations in a sport grappling with its evolving identity.

Allen Iverson's embrace of oversized clothes, throwback jerseys, and streetwear forged an unbreakable link to hip-hop culture, positioning him as a pivotal architect of early-2000s urban style amid a shifting cultural landscape. In the late '90s and into the new millennium, as hip-hop evolved from underground roots to global dominance—driven by labels like Roc-A-Fella and artists like Jay-Z—Iverson mirrored the genre's aesthetic ethos, donning baggy jeans that sagged with deliberate nonchalance, extra-large T-shirts cascading over his frame like canvases for bold graphics, and vintage jerseys honoring basketball legends while nodding to rap's reverence for heritage. This streetwear fusion wasn't superficial; it stemmed from Iverson's Hampton upbringing, where hip-hop served as soundtrack and survival guide, its oversized silhouettes symbolizing protection, swagger, and communal identity in Black urban spaces facing economic hardship and police scrutiny.

Socially aware observers recognized Iverson's look as resistance against the NBA's buttoned-up image, echoing hip-hop's anti-establishment vibe—baggy pants evoking the loose fits of breakdancers and graffiti artists, jerseys transforming into statements of cultural pride. His influence rippled outward, shaping early-2000s fashion: youth in cities from Philly to L.A. adopted the baggy era's uniform, blending sportswear with high-end street labels like Sean John, turning playground courts into runways. Historically grounded in the post-crack epidemic recovery of Black communities, Iverson's style democratized self-expression, making vulnerability visible through layers that concealed scars while projecting unassailable toughness. By the mid-2000s, his direct connection to hip-hop had normalized oversized aesthetics in mainstream culture, influencing everything from music videos to mall fashion, proving one athlete could redefine an era's visual language.

The league's unease simmered from the moment Iverson's cornrows and tattoos hit the hardwood, a palpable tension between his unfiltered authenticity and the NBA office's vision of a sanitized, corporate-friendly brand. In the late 1990s, under Commissioner David Stern, the NBA sought to expand its global appeal by emulating Michael Jordan's polished persona—suits, smiles, and marketability that appealed to suburban audiences and sponsors. Iverson's arrival disrupted this narrative, his hip-hop-infused style evoking urban Black experiences that the establishment viewed with suspicion, often framing it through coded language as "unprofessional" or a threat to the game's image. This discomfort wasn't abstract; it manifested in subtle pressures, like fines for dress violations and media narratives that amplified stereotypes of Black athletes as "thugs," rooted in broader societal anxieties about race and class during the post-Rodney King era.

Historically, the NBA had navigated similar waters, from Bill Russell's activism to the ABA's flair, but Iverson's defiance felt personal, his refusal to conform a direct challenge to Stern's empire-building. Socially aware critics noted the racial undertones—how authenticity for white players meant eccentricity, but for Black stars like Iverson, it invited scrutiny. Yet this friction highlighted deeper cultural shifts, as younger, diverse fans celebrated his realness, forcing the league to grapple with its evolving demographics. By the early 2000s, the seeds of resentment grew, setting the stage for formal interventions that would attempt to rein in the very expression Iverson championed.

Beneath the glossy veneer of sports journalism in the late 1990s and early 2000s lurked a media backlash against Iverson's style that often masked deeper racial undertones, framing his authenticity through coded criticism designed to police Black expression. Terms like "thug" surfaced repeatedly in columns and broadcasts, a loaded word evoking criminality and danger, applied to Iverson's cornrows and tattoos despite his on-court brilliance—echoing historical stereotypes that have long demonized Black men as threats rather than trailblazers. "Too urban" became another euphemism, subtly dismissing his hip-hop-infused aesthetic as incompatible with the NBA's corporate image, implying that elements rooted in Black street culture were inherently unrefined or disruptive, a narrative grounded in America's post-civil rights unease with unassimilated Black success.

"Unprofessional" rounded out the triad, a seemingly neutral critique that veiled bias against Iverson's refusal to conform to the Michael Jordan mold—tailored suits and subdued personas that appealed to white suburban fans and sponsors. Socially aware observers recognized these phrases as dog whistles, perpetuating systemic racism by questioning Iverson's legitimacy in a league built on Black talent yet marketed to broader audiences. Historically, this mirrored earlier eras, from Muhammad Ali's vilification to the ABA's marginalized flair, where Black innovation faced resistance. Yet in Black communities, such criticism fueled defense and pride, viewing Iverson as a cultural warrior whose "thug" label only amplified his role as a mirror for resilience amid marginalization. This backlash didn't dim his influence; it exposed the league's fractures, highlighting how style became a battleground for identity and power.

Across playgrounds and inner-city courts in the late 1990s and early 2000s, a generation of young fans latched onto Allen Iverson as a living mirror of their worlds, seeing in his every crossover and cornrow a validation of their music, neighborhoods, and core identities. For kids immersed in hip-hop's golden era—blasting tracks from Nas's Illmatic or OutKast's Aquemini— Iverson embodied the genre's unpolished truth, his arm sleeve and baggy shorts echoing the defiant flair of rappers who turned street struggles into anthems of empowerment. In neighborhoods scarred by economic neglect and over-policing, like those in South Philly or Compton, his Hampton-bred resilience resonated deeply, a symbol that someone from the block could storm the NBA's gates without shedding their essence, blending vulnerability from shared traumas like family hardships with the toughness forged in asphalt battles.

Socially, this embrace marked a cultural awakening, as Black and Latino youth, often marginalized in mainstream narratives, found pride in Iverson's refusal to code-switch—his tattoos and do-rags a badge of authenticity amid a society pushing assimilation. Historically rooted in the post-crack epidemic recovery, where hip-hop became a lifeline for expression, Iverson's image empowered them to claim space unapologetically, influencing everything from schoolyard fashion to dreams of breaking barriers. This connection wasn't superficial; it fostered a sense of belonging, turning Iverson into a cultural beacon who made their identities visible and viable on a global stage.

In the crucible of the NBA's spotlight, Iverson masterfully wove toughness with emotional transparency, a duality that redefined athletic self-expression and rippled through sports culture like a seismic wave. His swagger was unmistakable—the crossover that left defenders in dust, the glare after a bucket, the unyielding drive despite his undersized frame—embodying the unbreakable spirit honed in Hampton's harsh realities, where survival demanded an armor of bravado. Yet beneath that facade lay profound vulnerability: tattoos chronicling lost loved ones and inner demons, post-game interviews where tears flowed freely after defeats, and candid admissions of personal struggles, from family hardships to legal battles, exposing the human frailty often masked in professional sports.

This blend challenged the stoic archetype of athletes as invincible machines, rooted in hip-hop's lyrical honesty where rappers like Tupac bared souls amid bravado. Socially, it empowered Black athletes to embrace wholeness, validating emotional openness in communities where mental health discussions were taboo. Historically grounded in the late-'90s shift toward authentic narratives, Iverson's influence paved the way for later stars—LeBron James sharing personal stories, Kevin Durant addressing burnout—normalizing vulnerability without diminishing swagger. Fans in urban enclaves saw it as liberation, a cultural pivot that made athletes relatable icons, blending raw emotion with fierce resilience to humanize the game and inspire a generation to express unfiltered selves on and off the court.

The ripple effects of Iverson's trailblazing style cascaded into the next wave of NBA stars, who modeled their swagger, fashion, and personas after the iconoclastic guard, embedding his ethos into the league's evolving identity. Russell Westbrook, with his audacious outfits—vibrant prints, bold accessories, and a fearless mix of street and high fashion—echoed Iverson's unapologetic self-expression, turning pre-game tunnels into personal runways much like AI's hip-hop-infused arrivals. Dwyane Wade embraced tattoos as emotional narratives, his inked skin a canvas of family tributes and life lessons, blending vulnerability with the tough, charismatic persona Iverson popularized, while adding his own flair through tailored yet edgy suits that nodded to urban roots.

Carmelo Anthony channeled Iverson's street swagger on and off the court, his cornrows and oversized hoodies in early career years a direct homage, infusing his scoring prowess with the same defiant attitude that challenged norms. Kyrie Irving adopted the intricate braids and arm sleeves, his elusive handles mirroring Iverson's crossover while his outspoken persona reflected the emotional transparency AI brought to stardom. Even LeBron James, though more polished, cited Iverson's influence on authenticity, incorporating elements like visible tattoos and hip-hop collaborations into his brand.

This generational shift, rooted in Iverson's fusion of hip-hop culture and basketball, empowered players to reject conformity, fostering a league where personal style became a form of resistance and pride. Socially, it amplified Black voices, inspiring athletes from diverse backgrounds to own their narratives, turning vulnerability into strength and swagger into legacy.

Corporate America found itself at a crossroads in the late 1990s as Allen Iverson's meteoric rise forced brands to weigh the risks of his polarizing image against the lucrative rewards of his cultural magnetism. Sponsors hesitated, haunted by media portrayals that painted Iverson as a "thug"—a code for his unfiltered Black urban authenticity, complete with cornrows, tattoos, and hip-hop affiliations—fearing backlash from conservative consumers and suburban demographics who preferred the sanitized appeal of Michael Jordan. This dilemma was historically rooted in the post-civil rights corporate landscape, where Black athletes were often expected to assimilate to avoid alienating white audiences, echoing the struggles of figures like Muhammad Ali whose activism initially repelled endorsements. Socially, it highlighted racial double standards: Iverson's style, born from Hampton's hardships, was seen as a liability, yet his authenticity resonated deeply with a burgeoning youth market hungry for representation.

Yet the profit potential was undeniable. Iverson's influence tapped into the exploding hip-hop economy, where authenticity drove sales among urban consumers and Gen-Xers, promising billions in apparel and sneaker revenue. Brands like Reebok gambled big, signing him to a lifetime deal in 2001 despite the controversy, recognizing his ability to move product through sheer cultural relevance. This tension played out in boardrooms, where fear of reputational damage clashed with data showing Iverson's fanbase—predominantly young, diverse, and loyal—boosting bottom lines. Ultimately, embracing him proved prescient, as his image normalized streetwear in mainstream marketing, but not without exposing corporate America's uneasy dance with Black culture's raw power.

The partnership between Allen Iverson and Reebok, forged in 1996 when the brand signed the rookie phenom, transcended the realm of footwear to become a seismic cultural force that amplified hip-hop's influence on global style and identity. Iverson's debut signature shoe, the Reebok Question— with its bold hexalite cushioning and crossover appeal—mirrored his on-court flair, quickly adopted by urban youth who saw in its design a nod to street-ball resilience and hip-hop's audacious aesthetics. As the Answer series followed, each model embedded Iverson's ethos: tattoos inspiring graphics, cornrows influencing marketing campaigns that blended vulnerability with unbreakable swagger, turning sneakers into symbols of defiance against conformity.

By 2001, the lifetime deal—guaranteeing annual payments and a massive payout at age 55—solidified Reebok's bet on Iverson's authenticity, even amid media backlash labeling him "controversial." This wasn't mere endorsement; it was a cultural collaboration that empowered Black athletes to own their narratives, with Iverson's shoes dominating playgrounds, music videos, and fashion spreads, influencing artists like Jay-Z and fueling the baggy era's streetwear boom. Socially, it challenged corporate America's hesitance toward urban Black icons, proving profitability in genuineness—sales soared as fans embraced the shoes as badges of pride from marginalized neighborhoods. Historically rooted in hip-hop's commercial explosion, the deal reshaped sneaker culture, paving the way for athlete-brands that prioritize personal story over polish, leaving an indelible mark on how sports intersect with identity and rebellion.

In the vibrant pulse of Black communities during the late 1990s and early 2000s, Iverson's style reverberated like a bassline through barbershops, where clippers hummed amid heated debates over his cornrows and tattoos, symbols of unapologetic pride that sparked conversations on authenticity versus assimilation, turning these spaces into forums for cultural affirmation. Rap lyrics immortalized him as a totem of resilience—Jadakiss invoking his crossover in "We Gonna Make It" as a metaphor for street survival, while Post Malone's "White Iverson" paid homage to his swagger, blending basketball flair with hip-hop hustle, lines that echoed in cyphers and playlists as anthems of defiance. Hip-hop videos amplified the connection, with Iverson cameoing in clips like Jadakiss's tracks or inspiring visuals of baggy jerseys and arm sleeves, his aesthetic a blueprint for artists channeling urban grit into mainstream visuals.

In inner cities, from Philly's blocks to L.A.'s corners, Iverson stood as a beacon for youth navigating poverty and scrutiny, his oversized gear and rebellious vibe a mirror to their realities, fostering pride in roots that society often marginalized. On college campuses, Black students emulated his look—braids swaying in dorm rooms, throwback jerseys at parties—his blend of vulnerability and toughness inspiring a generation to claim space unyieldingly, turning campuses into extensions of the cultural revolution he ignited. This resonance wasn't fleeting; it wove Iverson into the fabric of Black identity, proving style could be a vessel for empowerment across everyday landscapes.

As the new millennium dawned, friction within the NBA's corridors of power intensified, with Commissioner David Stern and team owners viewing Iverson's burgeoning influence as a direct affront to the league's carefully curated image. His cornrows, tattoos, and hip-hop swagger, which electrified younger demographics, unnerved gatekeepers who favored the Jordan-era polish—clean lines, corporate endorsements, and an appeal to suburban white audiences that drove revenue. Stern, architect of the NBA's global expansion, subtly pressured for conformity, issuing fines for dress code violations and do-rag appearances, framing them as professionalism lapses while masking deeper discomfort with Black urban culture's intrusion into the sport. Owners, echoing this sentiment, worried about alienating sponsors; whispers in boardrooms labeled Iverson a "thug," a racially charged term that amplified stereotypes and justified scrutiny over his entourage and off-court style, rooted in fears that his authenticity might erode the league's marketability amid post-90s racial tensions.

Historically, this mounting pressure mirrored earlier battles, like the ABA's flamboyance being tamed by NBA mergers, but Iverson's case felt acutely personal, his refusal to assimilate a cultural insurgency that challenged ownership's control. Socially aware insiders noted the hypocrisy—white players' eccentricities were quirks, while Iverson's were threats—fueling resentment that simmered through the early 2000s. Yet this establishment pushback only amplified his legend, as fans rallied around his defiance, setting the stage for broader confrontations over identity and expression in professional sports.

Iverson's imprint on the NBA extended far beyond the threads of his jerseys or the ink on his skin, igniting a revolution that fundamentally altered how athletes claimed their identities and broadcast them to the world. By fusing hip-hop's raw authenticity with basketball's global stage, he dismantled the barriers of conformity, empowering players to weave personal histories—triumphs, scars, and cultural roots—into their public personas, turning vulnerability into a source of strength and swagger into a statement of self-sovereignty. This shift resonated globally, influencing not just American sports but international arenas where young athletes from diverse backgrounds began embracing styles that reflected their lived experiences, from braids in European soccer to tattoos in Asian leagues, challenging institutional norms that prioritized polish over truth. Socially, it amplified voices from marginalized communities, fostering a culture where Black excellence could thrive unfiltered, inspiring figures across disciplines to reject assimilation in favor of bold expression.

Yet this empowerment brewed tension, as the NBA's old guard eyed the changing landscape with growing alarm, whispers of a dress code circulating in boardrooms to rein in the very freedom Iverson had unleashed. Historically, his era marked a pivotal turn in sports culture, proving that identity wasn't accessory but essence, reshaping how generations viewed heroism—not in victories alone, but in the unapologetic embrace of self. Iverson didn't merely dress differently; he dressed the game in revolution, leaving a legacy that continues to echo through arenas worldwide.

Clashes, Critics, and Consequences

As Allen Iverson's star ascended in the early 2000s, catapulting him from a gritty Philadelphia underdog to the NBA's most electrifying force, fame refracted into a relentless, unforgiving glare. No longer just a player dissected for his crossovers and scoring bursts, Iverson became a cultural lightning rod, his every move amplified by a media ecosystem hungry for controversy. Where Michael Jordan's endorsements polished a pristine image, Iverson's spotlight exposed raw edges—his cornrows, tattoos sprawling like defiant graffiti, and hip-hop-infused wardrobe were framed not as personal expression but as threats to the league's polished facade. Critics in outlets like ESPN and major newspapers painted him as the archetype of urban excess, a "thug" whose authenticity clashed with the NBA's aspirations for mainstream appeal, often laced with unspoken racial undertones that equated Black street culture with unruliness.

The scrutiny burrowed deeper than box scores, invading his personal life with a ferocity reserved for tabloid scandals. His friendships with childhood crew from Hampton, Virginia, were scrutinized as potential liabilities, whispers of gang affiliations swirling despite his loyalty to roots that grounded him amid chaos. Fashion choices—baggy jeans, durags, and diamond chains—drew barbs implying delinquency, far beyond the mild rebukes faced by white counterparts for similar flair. Iverson's emotional outbursts, like the infamous 2002 "practice" rant, were stripped of context: delivered amid grief over his best friend Rahsaan Langeford's murder, it was edited into memes mocking his dedication, ignoring the vulnerability of a man mourning while performing under siege.

This media hostility wasn't mere coverage; it was a campaign that questioned his character, amplifying minor incidents—like a 2001 fine for derogatory remarks to hecklers—into indictments of his soul. Iverson, introspective in rare quiet moments, felt the weight: "The sh— hurt," he later reflected, acknowledging how false narratives pierced, especially as his children absorbed the rumors. Yet he drew lines, refusing to defend against petty judgments but vowing response to grave labels like "racist" or "molester." In this arena, fame didn't elevate; it isolated, turning Iverson into a symbol of resistance against an industry eager to sanitize its Black icons, exposing fractures in how America consumed its heroes. The pressure mounted, foreshadowing broader clashes yet to come.

Beneath the veneer of sports journalism in the early 2000s lurked a insidious undercurrent of racial bias, where critiques of Allen Iverson often masked deeper prejudices in coded language that echoed America's longstanding discomfort with unapologetic Black identity. Terms like "thug" or "gangster" were wielded not as descriptors of behavior but as shorthand for a perceived threat, transforming Iverson's cornrows and tattoos into symbols of urban menace rather than cultural pride. Commentators in outlets such as Sports Illustrated and The New York Times framed his hip-hop affiliations as evidence of moral decay, implying that his authenticity from Hampton's streets disqualified him from the NBA's genteel aspirations—a narrative rarely applied to white players like Jason Williams, whose flashy play earned nicknames like "White Chocolate" without the same venom. This subtle racism amplified fears of a league overrun by "streetballers," a euphemism laden with class and racial undertones, suggesting Iverson's style corrupted the game's purity.

The tension simmered in editorials questioning his "professionalism," a word that veiled expectations of assimilation into white corporate norms, dismissing Iverson's vulnerability—his grief, his loyalty—as excuses for unruliness. Black critics, too, grappled with this divide, some defending him as a cultural beacon while others worried his image reinforced stereotypes. Yet the scrutiny exposed a broader hypocrisy: Iverson's "rebellious" image fueled league profits through merchandise and viewership, even as it invited condemnation. Introspectively, this era revealed how media narratives policed Black expression, turning Iverson into a scapegoat for societal anxieties about race, class, and control. The pressure built, his every misstep dissected as proof of inherent flaws, foreshadowing institutional responses that would seek to rein in such defiance.

Allen Iverson's ascent invited a microscope that dissected not just his game but the very fabric of his existence, turning personal choices into public indictments. His fashion—oversized jerseys, durags, and jewelry that screamed street credibility—drew scorn from league traditionalists who viewed it as a rejection of professionalism, a far cry from the tailored suits of predecessors like Jordan. Critics lambasted his tattoos as badges of rebellion, symbols of a life too raw for the NBA's glossy image, often ignoring how they chronicled his hardships and triumphs. His friends, a tight-knit crew from Hampton's tough neighborhoods, were portrayed as enablers of chaos, their presence at games and events fueling narratives of gang ties and distractions, despite Iverson's insistence on loyalty as his anchor in a fickle world.

Music intertwined with this scrutiny; Iverson's hip-hop affiliations, including his brief rap career under the moniker Jewelz, were derided as glorifying violence and excess, clashing with the league's push for family-friendly appeal. Nightlife tales amplified the frenzy—reports of club appearances and late nights painted him as undisciplined, a partygoer whose energy off-court undermined his on-court brilliance, even as peers envied his unfiltered vibe. Yet it was his authenticity that ignited the deepest friction: unapologetic, layered with vulnerability from a turbulent youth, it exposed a cultural chasm. Iverson introspected on this burden, feeling the sting of being reduced to a stereotype while carrying the hopes of those who saw themselves in him. This relentless judgment not only strained his psyche but foreshadowed a league reckoning, where individual expression met institutional control head-on.

Allen Iverson never campaigned to be the vanguard of a revolution; he simply arrived in the NBA as himself, a 6-foot dynamo from Hampton's hardscrabble streets, and the league's cultural fault lines cracked wide open. By the early 2000s, his unfiltered authenticity—cornrows braided on the bench, tattoos etching stories of survival, baggy shorts and throwback jerseys blending hip-hop swagger with hardwood ferocity—positioned him as the unwitting emblem of a seismic shift, where Black urban expression invaded the NBA's sanitized arena. What began as personal style, rooted in poverty and resilience, morphed into a blueprint for player autonomy, inspiring a generation to embrace dreads, jewelry, and shooting sleeves without apology, transforming team tunnels into runways and challenging the Jordan-era polish.

Yet this unintended leadership exacted a toll, thrusting Iverson into a maelstrom of expectations as the face of disenfranchised youth and hip-hop's incursion into sports. Media scrutiny laced with racial bias branded him a "thug," misreading his durags and chains as threats rather than tributes to his roots, while league brass eyed his influence warily, foreshadowing crackdowns like the 2005 dress code aimed at curbing "gangsta" aesthetics. Introspectively, Iverson grappled with the burden: the emotional sting of scapegoating, the weight of representing communities amid personal scars from incarceration and loss, and the isolation of fame that demanded vulnerability while punishing it. He absorbed the hits—financial betrayals, bodily breakdowns, relational strains—quietly mourning the misunderstandings, even as his defiance exposed America's unease with unbridled Black identity. This pressure, layered with cultural divide, simmered toward an inevitable confrontation, where individual rebellion met institutional restraint.

Allen Iverson's unyielding authenticity clashed like thunder against the NBA's corporate machinery, a friction born from his refusal to sand down the rough edges of his identity for the sake of marketability. In an era when the league, under Commissioner David Stern, sought to project a polished, family-oriented image to attract sponsors and suburban fans, Iverson's cornrows, tattoos, and hip-hop swagger represented a direct affront. His baggy attire and durags weren't just style; they were declarations of self, rooted in the streets of Hampton, Virginia, and the cultural currents of Black America that the NBA's boardrooms viewed with suspicion. This defiance ignited tensions with team management, particularly in Philadelphia, where executives like Larry Brown and Billy King oscillated between harnessing his brilliance and reining in his perceived excesses—

demanding he conform to practice schedules and public personas that felt alien to his core.

The corporate side, obsessed with image control, saw Iverson as a liability: his emotional transparency, like the raw grief in press conferences, was spun as volatility, while his loyalty to old friends invited whispers of instability. Sponsors hesitated, endorsements trickled compared to peers, as brands favored the sanitized appeal of players who mirrored Jordan's corporate sheen. Introspectively, Iverson wrestled with this divide, his vulnerability surfacing in quiet admissions of hurt from misrepresentations, yet he doubled down, prioritizing truth over facade. This stance exposed the league's unease with unscripted Black excellence, amplifying racial and class divides. The pressure simmered, emotional tolls mounting—strained relationships, eroded trust—as Iverson bore the consequences of authenticity in a system bent on assimilation. Such frictions hinted at brewing institutional responses, where personal expression would soon face league-wide mandates.

In the heart of Philadelphia, where grit and defiance are woven into the city's blue-collar fabric, Allen Iverson emerged as more than a basketball savior—he became its living pulse, a role that exacted a profound emotional and psychological toll. The City of Brotherly Love, scarred by economic decline and racial tensions, saw in Iverson a mirror of its own resilience: an undersized warrior from poverty's grip, battling odds with unbridled ferocity. Yet embodying this identity meant shouldering expectations that transcended the court, transforming personal triumphs into communal victories and failures into collective heartbreaks. The 2001 NBA Finals run, where he dragged a scrappy Sixers squad to the brink against the Lakers, amplified this bond, fans chanting his name like a battle cry, but it also isolated him, the weight of a city's hopes pressing like an invisible yoke.

Psychologically, the burden manifested in quiet erosion—sleepless nights haunted by scrutiny, the sting of betrayals from those who profited off his image while questioning his worth. Iverson's vulnerability, rarely aired publicly, surfaced in introspective moments: the grief over lost friends compounded by the demand to perform as Philly's unbreakable icon, even as injuries ravaged his body and media narratives chipped at his spirit. Culturally aware observers noted the layered irony; as a Black man from Hampton's streets, he represented empowerment for marginalized communities, yet the pressure to "carry" Philadelphia often felt like a cage, reinforcing stereotypes while denying him space for frailty. Relationships strained under this glare—family dynamics frayed, friendships tested—as authenticity clashed with the pedestal's demands. The toll deepened fractures, emotional scars accumulating like tattoos on his skin, foreshadowing a broader reckoning where individual burdens met institutional forces.

Beneath the armored exterior of Allen Iverson's on-court bravado—the crossovers that humiliated defenders, the defiant stare-downs after impossible shots—lurked a fragility that few glimpsed amid the roar of arenas. The public saw The Answer: a cultural insurgent, cornrows flying, tattoos narrating battles won, his swagger a shield against a world that demanded conformity. Yet privately, the push-and-pull tore at him, a constant negotiation between the image he projected and the wounds he concealed. Grief shadowed his prime; the 2001 murder of his childhood friend Rahsaan Langeford shattered him, turning the infamous "practice" press conference into a raw outpouring misread as petulance, when it was really a cry from a man unraveling under loss and scrutiny.

Alcohol became a silent adversary, a crutch for the emotional voids left by a turbulent youth—incarceration at 17, family instability—that fame only amplified. Iverson's authenticity, so celebrated by fans who revered his unfiltered Blackness, masked deeper vulnerabilities: the fear of betrayal from hangers-on, the strain on his marriage to Tawanna Turner that would later erupt into divorce, and the psychological weight of representing a culture while battling personal demons. Introspectively, he wrestled with this duality, admitting in quieter reflections how the pedestal isolated him, how public adulation clashed with private despair. The swagger protected, but it also imprisoned, forcing him to perform invincibility even as injuries and heartaches eroded his core. This internal friction exposed the cost of being an icon in a league that prized polish over pain, hinting at systemic clashes on the horizon where vulnerability would be further suppressed.

The year 2002 emerged as a flashpoint in Allen Iverson's career, a confluence of incidents that thrust him deeper into the media's crosshairs and amplified narratives of instability. In April, shots rang out near a Philadelphia nightclub where Iverson lingered with friends, authorities later deeming him a potential target in a dispute that escalated from words to gunfire, though he escaped unharmed. The episode fueled whispers of his risky associations, with outlets framing it as evidence of a life courting danger, ignoring the vulnerability of being marked in his own city. Barely a month later, following the Sixers' playoff exit, Iverson's press conference devolved into the infamous "practice" tirade, where he repeated the word 22 times amid frustration over scrutiny of his absences—absences tied to mourning his slain friend. Media clips looped the outburst, stripping context to portray him as petulant and unprofessional, a Black athlete defiant against authority, while glossing over his grief.

Then, in July, domestic turmoil boiled over: Iverson, seeking his estranged wife Tawanna, allegedly burst into a cousin's apartment armed, threatening occupants in a haze of anger. Charges of assault and gun possession followed, later dismissed for lack of evidence, but the damage lingered. Tabloids and sports columns painted him as volatile, a "thug" whose street roots endangered the NBA's image, laced with racial subtext that equated his emotions with criminality. These controversies eroded endorsements, strained team dynamics, and deepened Iverson's introspection, the public armor cracking under private anguish. Yet they exposed a cultural rift, setting the stage for the league's tightening grip on player presentation.

As the early 2000s wore on, whispers in the NBA's corridors of power grew into murmurs of reform, a subtle but insistent push to reclaim the league's image from the cultural currents Allen Iverson had unleashed. David Stern, the commissioner whose vision had globalized basketball, eyed the shifting landscape with unease: players arriving in throwback jerseys, durags peeking from beneath caps, chains glinting under arena lights—a visual lexicon borrowed from hip-hop that, to boardroom sensibilities, evoked disorder rather than dynamism. Iverson's influence rippled outward, emboldening a new wave of athletes to infuse street authenticity into the sport's aesthetic, but this evolution clashed with the NBA's corporate ambitions, where sponsors craved relatability to middle America, not reminders of urban grit.

Introspectively, the tension revealed deeper fissures—racial and generational divides that positioned Iverson as the scapegoat for a league grappling with its own diversity. Executives convened quietly, debating how to "professionalize" appearances without alienating talent, their discomfort manifesting in memos and off-record briefings that hinted at mandates to come. Iverson, sensing the gathering storm, reflected on the irony: his style, once a personal armor forged in hardship, now threatened to provoke institutional backlash, straining his relationships with mentors and peers who navigated the same precarious line between self-expression and survival.

The pressure mounted, emotional undercurrents swirling as critics amplified calls for control, framing Iverson's defiance as a liability. Communities rallied around him, seeing the critique as an assault on Black cultural agency, while fans divided along lines of tradition versus innovation. Yet the league's machinery churned forward, policies crystallizing in response to this very friction, poised to enforce a uniformity that would redefine the boundaries of identity in the NBA. The air thickened with anticipation, a showdown looming where personal freedom would collide with enforced decorum.

Amid the swirling controversies enveloping Allen Iverson in the early 2000s, the NBA's fraternity revealed a generational rift in their responses, a tension that mirrored broader cultural debates about authenticity and assimilation. Younger players, many of whom entered the league idolizing his fearless style, rallied around him as a beacon of empowerment. LeBron James, still carving his own path, hailed Iverson as one of the most influential figures in basketball history, crediting his cornrows, crossover dribble, and unapologetic swagger for reshaping how athletes expressed themselves. James Harden echoed this sentiment, drawing parallels between the "negative energy" he endured and Iverson's scrutiny, positioning it as a badge of trailblazing. Others, like Stephen Jackson, conveyed deep personal reverence, emphasizing Iverson's irreplaceable role in the culture, especially after losses like Kobe Bryant's passing. These endorsements underscored a sense of solidarity, viewing the criticism not as personal failings but as attacks on Black cultural expression, inspiring a wave of emulation in tattoos, fashion, and attitude.

In contrast, older veterans often voiced reservations, their critiques laced with concerns over professionalism and the game's evolution. Charles Barkley dismissed Iverson's approach as that of a "playground rookie," implying immaturity, while Scottie Pippen faulted his shot selection as excessive for a point guard. Such barbs reflected a nostalgia for the Jordan-era decorum, where conformity bolstered marketability, and Iverson's defiance seemed disruptive. Yet even among elders, glimmers of defense emerged—Gilbert Arenas praised his relentless mentality, likening it to an underdog's unyielding hustle. This divide intensified introspection across locker rooms, players grappling with the emotional cost of navigating identity under scrutiny. As criticisms mounted, the league's unease coalesced, hinting at policies that would soon mandate a more controlled image, forcing everyone to choose sides.

The NBA's cultural battlefield in the early 2000s cleaved sharply between those who revered Allen Iverson as a liberating force and those who branded him a peril to the game's sanctity. Fans, particularly from urban enclaves and hip-hop circles, embraced him as a messiah of authenticity—a 6-foot rebel whose cornrows, tattoos, and unbridled swagger mirrored their own unfiltered lives. In Philadelphia's rowhouse neighborhoods and beyond, supporters donned Reebok Questions and arm sleeves, chanting his name as a rallying cry against assimilation. They saw his defiance not as disruption but as empowerment, a Black icon who dragged the league into the streets, making basketball accessible and electric for a generation weary of polished archetypes. His "practice" outburst, for them, wasn't petulance but a raw glimpse into the humanity critics ignored, fueling merchandise sales and arena fervor that proved his market pull.

Yet gatekeepers—media pundits, league executives, and traditionalists—viewed this surge with alarm, framing Iverson's influence as an erosion of professionalism. Outlets dissected his entourage and nightlife as harbingers of moral decay, racial subtext simmering in labels like "thug" that evoked fears of a league too Black, too urban for corporate sponsors. David Stern's administration whispered of image control, seeing Iverson's style as a liability that alienated suburban demographics, even as it boosted ratings. This divide exposed America's fractured gaze on Black excellence: fans celebrated the vulnerability beneath the bravado, while critics demanded conformity, their critiques laced with condescension toward his roots. Introspectively, the tension gnawed at the sport's soul, communities rallying around Iverson's unyielding self while institutions plotted countermeasures. The storm brewed, as policies were on the horizon to enforce a vision where expression bowed to decorum.

The NBA's corporate ecosystem, a labyrinth of endorsements and airbrushed narratives, recoiled from Allen Iverson's unvarnished edge, creating a tension that rippled through his career like a fault line under pressure. Sponsors, ever cautious of controversy, shied away from his image—Reebok stood as a rare loyalist with the Answer sneaker line, but giants like Nike and Gatorade opted for safer bets, players whose personas aligned with suburban appeal rather than street authenticity. Iverson's hip-hop affiliations and tattoos signaled risk to boardrooms attuned to Middle America's sensibilities, where racial undertones framed his style as alienating, not aspirational. This hesitation translated to lost millions, his marketability stunted despite on-court wizardry that filled arenas and boosted ratings, exposing the hypocrisy of a league profiting from his electricity while punishing its source.

Media coverage amplified this corporate chill, turning Iverson into a cautionary tale: headlines dissected his "practice" rant as evidence of immaturity, ignoring the grief fueling it, while tabloids sensationalized nightclub incidents as proof of instability. Culturally, this scrutiny layered on the burden, positioning him as a symbol of Black defiance that threatened the NBA's global brand, a narrative that deepened divides between urban fans and institutional gatekeepers. Business opportunities evaporated—potential ventures in music or apparel fizzled amid whispers of unreliability, straining his finances and relationships as betrayals from agents and partners mounted.

Introspectively, Iverson navigated this minefield with quiet resolve, his vulnerability clashing against the demand for conformity, the emotional scars accumulating like unpaid debts. Yet this friction illuminated a broader clash, where individual expression challenged profit-driven control, setting the stage for league interventions that would soon demand assimilation.

As the new millennium unfolded, the NBA found itself at a crossroads, with Allen Iverson unwittingly serving as the catalyst that illuminated deep-seated divides across generations, cultures, and racial lines. His infusion of hip-hop aesthetics—cornrows, baggy attire, and an unapologetic nod to street life—challenged the league's longstanding image of polished professionalism, a relic of the Bird-Magic-Jordan era that appealed to white, suburban audiences. Older commentators and veterans, steeped in traditions of conformity, decried this shift as a dilution of the game's integrity, their critiques often laced with generational disdain for what they saw as youthful excess. In media circles, outlets like Sports Illustrated and network broadcasts amplified these voices, framing Iverson's style as a threat to marketability, exposing a cultural chasm where urban Black expression clashed with corporate expectations.

Racially, the scrutiny peeled back layers of bias: Iverson's authenticity, drawn from Hampton's marginalized communities, was coded as "thuggish" or "unprofessional," terms rarely leveled at white players with similar flair. This narrative highlighted America's unease with unbridled Black identity in sports, where media gatekeepers—predominantly white—policed boundaries, while younger fans and players from diverse backgrounds celebrated him as a liberator. The divide widened in locker rooms and living rooms alike, with hip-hop generation athletes embracing tattoos and durags as empowerment, contrasting sharply with elders' calls for assimilation. Introspectively, this friction forced a reckoning, Iverson's presence a mirror reflecting societal fractures, the emotional undercurrents of isolation and defiance simmering beneath. Yet as debates intensified, the league's discomfort coalesced, hinting at impending policies to bridge—or enforce—these rifts through mandated decorum.

As the controversies swirled and the cultural fissures deepened, the NBA's brass began to stir in the shadows, their unease coalescing into something more deliberate—a calculated response to the unbridled expression that Allen Iverson had come to embody. David Stern, the architect of the league's global ascent, watched with mounting concern as hip-hop's influence seeped into every facet of the game: from the tunnel walks turned fashion statements to the tattoos that narrated stories of survival, all challenging the sanitized narrative sold to sponsors and broadcasters. Whispers in executive suites turned to strategy sessions, where the term "professionalism" masked a desire to reclaim control, to temper the raw authenticity that appealed to urban youth but alienated conservative demographics. Iverson's presence had exposed the league's vulnerabilities—racial biases baked into critiques, generational clashes over identity, and a fanbase split between adoration and apprehension.

Introspectively, this buildup carried a tense inevitability, the air thick with the knowledge that change was coming, not as evolution but as enforcement. Players murmured in locker rooms, sensing the shift; communities braced for what felt like an assault on cultural agency. The dress code, still in draft form by 2004, loomed as the first salvo—a policy mandating business casual attire, banning chains, durags, and throwbacks, ostensibly to foster respectability but unmistakably aimed at curbing the "thug" aesthetic critics pinned on Iverson. It would mark the league's institutional pivot, a line drawn in the sand against the very forces he unleashed, promising a showdown where personal freedom clashed with corporate decree. The era of unchecked swagger teetered on the brink, a major realignment poised to redefine the boundaries of self in the NBA.

Trade Drama & Evolution

The aftermath of the 2001 NBA Finals hung over the Philadelphia 76ers like a persistent fog, a mix of pride and profound disappointment that seeped into every corner of the organization. Allen Iverson had led the team to the brink of immortality, earning MVP honors with 31.1 points per game and dragging a gritty, undersized squad past Milwaukee and Toronto in epic seven-game series, only to fall in five to the juggernaut Lakers. The step-over of Tyronn Lue in Game 1 became an iconic symbol of defiance, but the loss left scars—Iverson's body battered from carrying the load, his spirit wrestling with what-ifs in a city that demanded championships. As confetti fell on Shaq and Kobe in Los Angeles, the emotional comedown hit hard back in Philly, where fans who had roared through the playoffs now faced the sobering reality of a roster built for one magical run, not sustained dominance.

Early signs of frustration surfaced almost immediately in the 2001-02 season, as the Sixers stumbled to a 43-39 record, scraping into the playoffs as the sixth seed with an offense ranked 26th in the league despite Iverson's relentless 31.4 points, 5.5 assists, and 4.5 rebounds per game. Injuries plagued Iverson, limiting him to 60 games, while the defense that had defined their Finals push held strong but couldn't compensate for inconsistent scoring from supporting cast like Eric Snow and Aaron McKie. Tensions with coach Larry Brown escalated, his demands for discipline clashing with Iverson's freewheeling style—critiques on shot selection, passing, and practice habits bubbling into public spats that hinted at deeper rifts. The high of June gave way to a tense locker room, where reflections on missed opportunities fueled a growing sense of instability. Iverson, ever the emotional lightning rod, internalized the blame, his reflective moments revealing a man haunted by the fragility of success in a league that moved on quickly. The cracks were there, small at first, but widening under the weight of unmet expectations in a pressure-cooker city.

The pressure within the Philadelphia 76ers organization mounted like a storm gathering over the Schuylkill River, transforming the euphoria of the 2001 Finals into a grinding weight of unmet expectations. Management, led by general manager Billy King and owner Ed Snider, had tasted the brink of a championship and now demanded sustained excellence, pouring resources into roster tweaks that failed to recapture the magic—trades for aging veterans like Derrick Coleman and Keith Van Horn aimed to bolster the lineup, but the team hovered around mediocrity, finishing seasons with records barely above .500. The front office's impatience clashed with the reality of an aging core and injury-prone stars, creating a tense atmosphere where every loss amplified whispers of rebuilds and shake-ups.

At the heart of the strain was the volatile dynamic between Allen Iverson and coach Larry Brown, a mentorship frayed by ideological battles: Brown's rigid emphasis on fundamentals, defense, and practice clashed with Iverson's improvisational brilliance and aversion to structured routines, leading to heated confrontations that spilled into the public eye. Brown's benchings and critiques, like sidelining Iverson in crunch time during games, fueled resentment, while Iverson's defiant responses highlighted a deeper rift between old-school discipline and the emerging street-ball ethos he embodied. The weight of those unmet goals—playoff exits in the first or second round year after year—bore down on everyone, eroding morale in the locker room and forcing reflective moments where Iverson pondered his role as the franchise's emotional anchor amid growing instability. This internal turmoil mirrored the league's broader push for conformity, as seen in the dress code debates, underscoring how personal freedoms were sacrificed under organizational pressures.

The partnership between Allen Iverson and Larry Brown, once a combustible force that propelled the Sixers to the 2001 Finals, reignited into volatility as exhaustion set in from years of high-stakes battles. Brown's relentless coaching style, honed through decades of demanding precision and discipline, began to wear on Iverson, whose raw, improvisational talent thrived on instinct rather than regimen. Post-Finals, the expectations in Philadelphia escalated—fans and management craved rings, not just runs—amplifying every misstep. Iverson's injuries and the team's inconsistent play fueled Brown's frustrations, leading to public criticisms of his star's shot selection and commitment. The emotional toll mounted; Iverson, reflective in quieter moments, felt the weight of being the franchise's heartbeat, while Brown, exhausted by the constant push-pull, questioned if their dynamic could endure. This strain echoed the league's broader clampdown on individuality, like the dress code that Iverson saw as another attempt to box in his free spirit, mirroring Brown's efforts to mold him.

Personality differences pushed them to a breaking point, with Brown's old-school authoritarianism clashing against Iverson's defiant, street-forged independence. Incidents piled up: benchings during games sparked Iverson's ire, and the infamous 2002 "practice" rant—triggered by grief over a lost friend and simmering resentments—exposed the raw fracture. Iverson's outburst, tense and unfiltered, wasn't just about skipping sessions but a cry against the unrelenting scrutiny and expectations that defined their bond. Brown, ever the taskmaster, viewed it as insubordination, deepening the rift that had simmered since Iverson's rookie days. Yet, amid the chaos, reflections on their shared successes hinted at mutual respect, even as the instability foreshadowed an inevitable split, testing Iverson's loyalty in a city that both revered and pressured him.

The first whispers of a trade emerged in the shadows of the 2002 offseason, subtle at first, like murmurs in the back rooms of the league's executive suites. Fresh off the infamous practice rant that exposed the deepening fissures between Iverson and Larry Brown, reports trickled out about Philadelphia's front office exploring options to move their star guard. Iverson, sensing the unease, dared the organization to pull the trigger, his bravado masking the emotional sting of potential betrayal in a city he had bled for. These early rumors were quiet, confined to insider columns and talk radio speculation, often tied to Iverson's defiant persona clashing with the NBA's growing emphasis on polish and conformity—echoed in the looming dress code debates that questioned players like him. The league buzzed faintly about possible deals to contenders like Detroit, where Iverson's scoring could pair with defensive anchors, but nothing materialized, leaving a tense undercurrent in Philly.

As seasons wore on, the whispers grew into a steady roar, amplified by the Sixers' persistent mediocrity and Iverson's mounting frustrations. By 2004, rumors escalated with talks of a swap to the Los Angeles Clippers, shaking the fanbase and forcing Iverson to confront the business realities of basketball. Media outlets dissected every non-committal statement from GM Billy King, while Iverson's reflective silences hinted at the toll—disappointment eroding his loyalty amid endless speculation. The pressure cooker of Philadelphia fed the frenzy, with fans debating his future on message boards and call-in shows. By 2006, the noise was deafening; Iverson's public trade demand turned whispers into headlines, testing his bond with the franchise as suitors like Denver circled, setting the stage for an inevitable upheaval in a career defined by resilience against instability.

The trade speculation that dogged Allen Iverson during his Philadelphia tenure carved deep emotional grooves into his psyche, challenging the very foundations of his loyalty to a city and franchise that had become extensions of his identity. From the early whispers in 2000, when a near-deal to Detroit fell through, Iverson felt a raw betrayal—here he was, the MVP pouring his soul into the Sixers, only to be treated as a commodity in boardroom negotiations. This stung his sense of loyalty, forged in the streets where bonds were unbreakable, making him question if his sacrifices—endless nights on the court, stepping over Lue in defiance—meant anything in the cold calculus of NBA business. The rumors amplified his fatigue, a bone-deep exhaustion from carrying the team's hopes while battling injuries and scrutiny, turning every press conference into a minefield where he masked vulnerability with bravado. Anger simmered beneath it all, erupting in moments like the 2002 practice rant, where grief over a murdered friend intertwined with fury at the constant trade talk, his voice cracking as he lashed out against the hurt inflicted on him and his family. Iverson's identity as the unapologetic rebel, already under siege from the league's dress code push for conformity, felt further eroded; he wasn't just a player but a cultural force, yet the speculation reduced him to trade bait, fueling reflective nights where disappointment morphed into resolve. Amid the tension, this instability forced an evolution, testing his resilience as the whispers grew louder, hinting at a fracture that loyalty alone couldn't mend.

The cold reality of the NBA as a business loomed over Allen Iverson like an unyielding shadow, stripping away the illusions of brotherhood that had defined his bond with Philadelphia. In a league where players were assets on balance sheets, Iverson's fierce loyalty—tattooed into his skin and poured out on the court—clashed violently with the front office's pragmatic decisions. Trades weren't personal vendettas but calculated moves to manage salaries, chase draft picks, and rebuild rosters, yet for Iverson, they felt like betrayals of the blood he had spilled for the Sixers. The dress code policy exemplified this corporate chill, a top-down mandate from Commissioner Stern that targeted Iverson's hip-hop aesthetic, forcing him into suits that symbolized conformity over camaraderie. As rumors swirled, Iverson reflected on his journey from Hampton's streets to Philly's icon, where fans chanted his name like a brother, only to see management weigh his value in trade talks. The tension built, his anger simmering against the fatigue of being commodified, highlighting how the NBA's business machinery ground down even its most passionate souls.

This clash tested Iverson's sense of brotherhood, a code of loyalty rooted in his upbringing that Philadelphia's blue-collar ethos had amplified. He had given everything—enduring injuries, criticism, and the weight of expectations—for a city that mirrored his grit, yet the league's realities exposed the fragility of that bond. Near-trades, like the 2000 Detroit deal that collapsed, left him reeling, disappointment etching deeper lines of distrust. Iverson's evolution amid this instability revealed a man grappling with the NBA's duality: a platform for dreams that doubled as a ruthless enterprise. The dress code battles foreshadowed broader conflicts, where personal identity bowed to market demands, forcing Iverson to confront whether loyalty could survive in a world prioritizing profits over people. As the pressure mounted, the inevitable pull toward change loomed, underscoring the heartbreaking divide between business and the brotherhood he cherished.

The media feeding frenzy around Allen Iverson's trade rumors transformed Philadelphia into a cauldron of speculation, where every whisper ignited headlines that dissected his future with relentless intensity. From the 2000 near-miss deal to Detroit, ESPN blared "Iverson's pulse in Philly is day-to-day," painting a picture of a star on life support amid organizational discord. Debates raged on talk shows and sports pages— was Iverson the defiant hero elevating a middling team, or the chaotic force holding it back? Non-rumors fueled the chaos too; quiet stretches amplified scrutiny, with outlets like the Philadelphia Inquirer probing his practice habits and off-court life, linking them to the league's dress code crackdown that cast Iverson as the poster child for rebellion. The emotional undercurrent was tense, as reporters chased leaks from GM Billy King, turning press conferences into battlegrounds where Iverson's reflective pauses hinted at inner turmoil. Fans devoured the drama, debating loyalty versus wins on radio call-ins, while national pundits on ESPN's "Pardon the Interruption" weighed his trade value against his cultural impact.

As rumors crescendoed in 2006, the frenzy hit fever pitch, with headlines like "All but over for Iverson" from the Pocono Record signaling an impending end. Chaos ensued as reports of deals to Denver or Boston flooded airwaves, sparking heated debates over his legacy—CBS News lamented it as a "tragedy," while others celebrated a fresh start. Non-stories, like stalled negotiations, only heightened the tension, with media outlets speculating on Iverson's anger and fatigue. The dress code saga intertwined, as pundits argued his non-conformity made him expendable in a polished NBA. Philadelphia's streets buzzed with uncertainty, fans oscillating between despair and resignation, reflecting the broader instability that forced Iverson's evolution amid the relentless spotlight.

The near-trades that haunted Allen Iverson's tenure with the Philadelphia 76ers exposed the fragility of his bond with the franchise, moments where loyalty teetered on the edge of corporate maneuvering. In the summer of 2000, just as Iverson was ascending to superstar status, a four-team deal nearly shipped him to the Detroit Pistons in exchange for Grant Hill and others, including Matt Geiger heading out with him. The agreement was reportedly in place, poised to reshape the Eastern Conference, but it unraveled over contract details and player approvals, leaving Iverson in Philly amid a swirl of tension. This close call amplified his reflective doubts about the NBA's business underbelly, where even an emerging icon like him—whose street-style flair would later clash with the 2005 dress code—could be bartered like a commodity. The emotional strain was palpable; Iverson, fresh off a breakout season, felt the fatigue of uncertainty, his anger simmering as the league's expectations for conformity mirrored the instability threatening his home.

Years later, as frustrations mounted, more brushes with departure intensified the drama. In 2006, before the draft, the Sixers came perilously close to trading Iverson to the Boston Celtics in a three-team swap that also involved the Denver Nuggets, only for negotiations to collapse at the eleventh hour. Around the same time, whispers of a deal to the Miami Heat surfaced, with Udonis Haslem later revealing he was nearly part of the package heading to Philadelphia. These near-misses deepened Iverson's sense of betrayal, testing his identity as Philly's defiant son amid the organization's roster shifts and the league's push for polished images. The tension built like a storm, forcing an evolution in Iverson—a man grappling with disappointment and loyalty—as the whispers of change foreshadowed the inevitable break that would soon come.

Philadelphia's fans, a passionate breed forged in the city's blue-collar grit, reacted to the swirling trade rumors around Allen Iverson with a volatile mix of fear and disbelief, as if the very soul of their franchise was being auctioned off. From the early whispers in 2000, when a deal to Detroit nearly materialized, supporters flooded talk radio and message boards with anxious pleas, terrified of losing the undersized warrior who embodied their defiant spirit. This fear intertwined with the NBA's dress code crackdown, which many saw as an attack on Iverson's authenticity—the cornrows, tattoos, and jewelry that mirrored the streets fans revered—amplifying worries that the league and Sixers brass were eager to purge his rebellious image. Disbelief set in as seasons dragged on without contention, with fans clinging to memories of the 2001 Finals run, unable to fathom trading the MVP who had stepped over Lue and poured his heart into every crossover. Yet, beneath the denial simmered anger, directed at management for failing to build around him, turning loyalty into a tense standoff where banners reading "Don't Trade AI" waved amid boos for lackluster play.

As rumors crescendoed in 2006, heartbreak enveloped the city like a heavy fog, fracturing the unbreakable bond between Iverson and his adopted home. Fans' loyalty shone through in sold-out arenas, where chants of "MVP" echoed even during slumps, but the disappointment bred resentment toward the front office, with some vowing to abandon the team if the trade went through. The emotional toll was profound—anger at the business machinations that commodified their icon, reflective sorrow over wasted primes, and a tense anticipation of loss that mirrored Iverson's own fatigue. In this pressure cooker, the dress code saga symbolized broader instability, pushing fans to confront how the NBA's corporate sheen threatened the raw connection they cherished, setting the stage for an inevitable parting laced with enduring heartbreak.

Allen Iverson navigated the swirling trade rumors with a public poise that masked the storm raging within, a delicate balance honed from years of scrutiny in Philadelphia's unforgiving spotlight. On the surface, he projected unflinching professionalism—fielding reporters' questions with measured responses, emphasizing his commitment to the Sixers even as whispers of deals to Detroit or Denver grew louder. During the 2000 offseason, when a near-trade left him reeling, Iverson publicly downplayed the drama, focusing on his MVP-caliber play and rallying fans with his on-court intensity. This facade extended to the league's dress code battles, where he voiced opposition calmly in interviews, framing it as a cultural issue rather than personal rebellion, all while suiting up as required to avoid fines. Yet, this composure was a shield; Iverson's reflective nature revealed in quieter moments how the speculation chipped away at his trust, forcing him to confront the NBA's business side that clashed with his deep-seated loyalty. The tension built, his public smiles hiding the fatigue of constant uncertainty, as he evolved from defiant star to a man weighing his worth amid organizational shifts.

Privately, the turmoil boiled over, a cauldron of frustration, anger, and emotional exhaustion that trade talks ignited. Iverson confided how the rumors drained him and his family, turning home life into a battleground of doubt and disappointment—feelings hurt by the Sixers' attempts to move him, as if his sacrifices meant little. Behind closed doors, away from the media frenzy, he grappled with betrayal, his guarded soul exposed in raw outbursts to close friends, echoing the grief-fueled "practice" rant that hinted at deeper pains. The dress code amplified this inner conflict, symbolizing a league intent on erasing his identity, fueling private reflections on conformity versus authenticity. As the instability mounted, Iverson's private frustrations spurred personal growth, tempering his anger into resilience, but the toll foreshadowed an inevitable fracture, where loyalty bowed to the pull of change.

The shifting roster pieces around Allen Iverson reflected the Philadelphia 76ers' desperate attempts to recapture the 2001 Finals magic, but each move only heightened the tension and instability within the organization. In the 2002 offseason, the front office traded away defensive anchor Dikembe Mutombo to the New Jersey Nets for Keith Van Horn and Todd MacCulloch, a decision aimed at adding offensive firepower but one that eroded the team's gritty identity, leaving Iverson to shoulder even more of the load amid growing frustrations. Larry Brown's departure in 2003 marked a seismic organizational shift, his resignation after six years of molding Iverson into an MVP signaling exhaustion from their volatile dynamic; Randy Ayers stepped in as head coach but was fired after 52 games with a dismal 21-31 record, replaced interim by Chris Ford as the Sixers missed the playoffs for the first time in Iverson's era. The 2003 offseason brought free-agent signings of Glenn Robinson and Kenny Thomas to bolster scoring, yet chemistry issues persisted, amplifying Iverson's reflective disappointment in a franchise that seemed to chase quick fixes rather than sustained vision. These changes, set against the league's dress code push for conformity, underscored how the NBA's business demands clashed with Iverson's unyielding style, forcing him to evolve amid the chaos.

Further reshuffling deepened the emotional strain, as the 2004 draft selection of Andre Iguodala introduced youthful potential, but the mid-2004-05 season acquisition of Chris Webber from the Sacramento Kings—trading away Corliss Williamson, Brian Skinner, and Kenny Thomas—proved a mismatched gamble, with Webber's injuries and declining mobility clashing with Iverson's up-tempo game. Jim O'Brien's hiring as coach in 2004 brought a brief playoff return, but his firing after one season due to front-office tensions paved the way for Maurice Cheeks in 2005, a former Sixer whose familiarity offered hope yet failed to stem the slide into a 38-44 record. Organizational decisions under GM Billy King prioritized cap flexibility and veteran additions, but the constant turnover bred fatigue and uncertainty, testing Iverson's loyalty as he pondered his role in a team perpetually in flux. This instability, mirrored in the dress code's assault on individuality, propelled Iverson's personal growth, transforming disappointment into a tense resolve as the whispers of his own departure grew inevitable.

Allen Iverson found himself ensnared in the limbo of the Philadelphia 76ers' shifting eras, a star whose identity was inextricably woven into a franchise teetering between faded glory and uncertain rebirth. The 2001 Finals run lingered as a haunting pinnacle, where Iverson's MVP brilliance and defiant step-over had electrified a city, but by the mid-2000s, the team's transition toward youth and cap flexibility left him adrift, his prime years clashing with a rebuild that sidelined his veteran fire. Trade rumors, from the near-miss Detroit deal in 2000 to escalating whispers in 2006, amplified his sense of being stuck—hurt and mad at the betrayal, as he admitted the speculation took a toll, eroding the loyalty that defined him. Iverson's reflective moments revealed a man grappling with exhaustion, his street-forged persona—cornrows, tattoos, and hip-hop flair—now under assault from the NBA's 2005 dress code, which he viewed as a direct attack on his authenticity, stereotyping him as the rebel who needed taming. This policy symbolized the league's push for conformity, mirroring the Sixers' own pivot away from his era, leaving him tense between nostalgia for past triumphs and dread of a future without him.

As the franchise reshuffled rosters—trading away anchors like Mutombo and bringing in mismatches like Webber—Iverson's frustration deepened, his daring challenges to management in 2002 exposing raw anger at being commodified amid the transition. His identity, once the heartbeat of Philly's grit, now felt like a relic in a team eyeing the horizon, forcing an emotional evolution where disappointment forged resilience. The dress code's hardships, which he endured as a badge of counterculture, paralleled this personal shift, pushing him to reflect on how his unapologetic style had reshaped the NBA yet trapped him in a narrative of obsolescence. In this pressure cooker, Iverson's loyalty wavered under the weight of instability, his private turmoil hinting at an inevitable departure that would sever ties to the past while propelling him—and the franchise—into uncharted futures.

The years of trade rumors and organizational upheaval forced Allen Iverson to evolve in profound ways, transforming him from a brash, individualistic scorer into a more nuanced leader amid the Sixers' crumbling foundation. As tensions with Larry Brown peaked in 2002, culminating in the raw "practice" rant that exposed his grief and frustrations, Iverson began reflecting on his role, recognizing the need to channel his defiance into mentorship. By 2003, with Brown gone and Iverson named team captain, he grew into a mature presence, prioritizing team flow over solo heroics—his assists climbed to 6.8 per game that season, a career high, as he adapted his frenetic style to uplift teammates like Glenn Robinson. The emotional toll of speculation, which he admitted wore on him and his family, fueled this shift, pushing him to lead by example in a locker room rife with instability. Yet, the NBA's 2005 dress code policy tested this growth, compelling Iverson to comply outwardly while voicing opposition, evolving his leadership into a cultural advocacy that resonated beyond the court, defending authenticity against corporate conformity.

As a competitor, Iverson's fire intensified through adversity, his scoring averages hovering above 30 points even amid injuries and roster flux, but he honed a sharper resilience, learning to conserve energy and make smarter plays in crunch time. Personally, the constant uncertainty—near-trades, media scrutiny, and Philadelphia's pressure—forged a deeper introspection, tempering his anger into quiet resolve as he confronted loyalty's limits in a business-driven league. The dress code saga mirrored this personal evolution, symbolizing his battle against erasure, turning disappointment into a reflective strength that prepared him for change. Amid the conflict, Iverson emerged wiser, his unbreakable spirit hinting at a future beyond Philly, where transformation awaited on the horizon.

The inevitable drift toward Allen Iverson's departure from Philadelphia settled over the Sixers like a slow-moving fog, thick with unspoken tensions and unfulfilled promises that made the end feel predestined, even as the final break lingered just out of sight. By late 2006, the trade rumors had evolved from fleeting whispers to a constant hum, amplified by Iverson's public demand for a move after a string of losses and benchings under Maurice Cheeks. The dress code policy, implemented a year earlier, had already signaled the league's discomfort with his unfiltered persona, forcing him into a reluctant compliance that mirrored the broader erosion of his fit within the franchise—a star whose cultural revolution clashed with a team eyeing a softer, more marketable rebuild. Fans sensed it in the subdued cheers at the Wachovia Center, where Iverson's heroics once ignited pandemonium but now carried a bittersweet edge, reflective of a city bracing for loss. The emotional weight pressed on Iverson, his fatigue manifesting in sharper edges during interviews, where loyalty warred with disappointment, hinting at a man ready to embrace change amid the instability that had defined his prime.

Yet, the writing on the wall wasn't scrawled in bold strokes but etched gradually through roster churns, media dissections, and the NBA's shifting tides, creating a tense anticipation that transformation was unavoidable. Iverson's evolution—as a leader mentoring Andre Iguodala, as a competitor adapting his game—couldn't halt the drift; instead, it underscored how his era in Philly had peaked, leaving him caught in a franchise's transition. The dress code battles, symbolic of larger conflicts over identity and conformity, foreshadowed this parting, pushing Iverson toward reflections on legacy beyond one city. As negotiations with Denver intensified behind closed doors, the air thickened with inevitability, a quiet acknowledgment that the unbreakable bond was fraying, setting the stage for a new chapter where both Iverson and the Sixers would redefine themselves in the wake of separation.

As the shadows lengthened over Allen Iverson's time in Philadelphia, the emotional stakes mounted like a gathering storm, each trade rumor and roster shuffle chipping away at the foundation of an era defined by his unyielding defiance. The dress code policy, a lingering symbol of the NBA's push for sanitized stardom, had already forced Iverson to confront how his cultural imprint—cornrows swaying, tattoos narrating survival—clashed with the league's corporate evolution, mirroring the Sixers' own drift toward a rebuild that sidelined his prime. Fans felt the pull, their loyalty fracturing into quiet heartbreak, whispering of a city losing its most authentic voice amid the pressure cooker of unmet championships. Iverson, reflective in the quiet hours, wrestled with the fatigue of carrying a franchise through instability, his anger tempered by a growing acceptance that loyalty had its limits in basketball's ruthless business. The tension built, cultural ripples from his style influencing a generation while the hardwood realities—playoff droughts, coaching carousels—signaled an impending rupture, preparing the ground for a shift that would redefine his legacy beyond Philly's borders.

In this precarious limbo, the basketball stakes loomed largest, with Iverson's evolution as a leader unable to halt the inevitable slide toward separation. The near-trades and media frenzies had forged him into a resilient competitor, yet the organization's pivot to youth like Andre Iguodala hinted at a future without his crossover magic, a major transformation brewing where cultural authenticity met institutional change. The dress code's constraints foreshadowed this broader upheaval, pushing Iverson toward a reflective crossroads where disappointment birthed resolve. As whispers of Denver solidified into negotiations, the air thickened with inevitability, the end of an era not as a sudden break but a slow, tense unraveling, leaving Philadelphia—and Iverson—poised on the edge of reinvention.

The Denver Turn & Late Career Shift

The news hit like a blindside crossover, leaving Allen Iverson reeling in a haze of disbelief and heartache. After a decade in Philadelphia, where he had poured his soul into every dribble and defiance, the Sixers finally severed the cord on December 19, 2006. Trade rumors had swirled for months, chipping away at his spirit, as Iverson later reflected on how they drained him emotionally, not just as a player but as a man grappling with uncertainty. The city that had crowned him its rebellious king now cast him aside, trading him to the Denver Nuggets along with Ivan McFarlin for Andre Miller, Joe Smith, and two first-round draft picks. For Iverson, it wasn't just a business transaction; it was a rupture of identity. Philadelphia had been his battleground, where his tattoos, cornrows, and unyielding swagger challenged the league's polished facade. Leaving meant confronting the fragility of loyalty in the NBA, a league that valued production over passion. Fans mourned with protests and jerseys burned in effigy, while Iverson internalized the pain, his eyes betraying a vulnerability rarely seen amid his armored exterior. Analytically, the move made sense for a rebuilding Sixers team tired of the drama, but emotionally, it marked the end of an era, forcing Iverson to reckon with a future untethered from the only home he'd known in the pros. The trade underscored how even icons like him were expendable, a harsh lesson in the commodification of talent that left scars deeper than any on-court defeat.

Shock rippled through the basketball world as Iverson boarded a plane for Denver, a city as foreign to his East Coast roots as the thin mountain air was to his lungs. At 31, he arrived amid hype and skepticism, his 31.2 points per game average trailing him like a ghost of dominance past. The Nuggets, led by young star Carmelo Anthony, saw him as the missing piece for a championship push, but Iverson felt the disorientation of displacement. Denver's laid-back vibe clashed with Philly's gritty intensity; gone were the familiar streets and adoring crowds that fueled his fire. Instead, he faced a new coach in George Karl, whose structured system demanded adaptation from a player accustomed to freelancing. Iverson's first press conference revealed a mix of excitement and guarded optimism, his words measured as he spoke of fresh starts. Yet beneath it lay the sting of rejection, a reminder that his individualism, once celebrated, now labeled him a liability. Analysts debated whether this was a rebirth or a demotion, with some predicting clashes in a backcourt built for scoring but suspect on defense. Emotionally, Iverson wrestled with the void, no longer the unquestioned alpha but a co-star in someone else's story. The trade's immediacy forced quick introspection, blending gratitude for a new opportunity with the ache of what was lost. In Denver, he sought to redefine himself, proving that his heart could beat just as fiercely at altitude, even as the league whispered doubts about his fit in an evolving game.

Adjusting to Denver proved a multifaceted challenge, as Iverson navigated the cultural and personal shifts of a new environment. The city's vibrant but unfamiliar scene—mountains instead of urban sprawl—mirrored his internal upheaval. Teammates like Marcus Camby and J.R. Smith welcomed him, but building chemistry took time, especially in Karl's offense that emphasized ball movement over isolation heroics. Iverson, ever the quick study, averaged 24.8 points and 7.2 assists in his first partial season, showing flashes of integration. Off the court, he grappled with relocation's loneliness, missing the familial bonds of Philly's tight-knit community. His family joined him eventually, but the transition highlighted his resilience, forged in harder times. Analytically, Denver's pace suited his speed, allowing crossover drives that still left defenders in dust. Yet emotionally, the move evoked a sense of impermanence, a star dimmed by change. Iverson's cornrows and arm sleeve became symbols of continuity amid flux, reminding fans of his cultural imprint. The Nuggets' playoff berth that year, though short-lived, validated the experiment, but Iverson's adjustment revealed deeper layers: a man learning to share the spotlight without losing his essence. In this phase, he tapped into mentorship, guiding younger players with stories of perseverance, blending his street-wise wisdom with the demands of a new system. It was a period of growth, where vulnerability met determination, setting the stage for unexpected partnerships.

The pairing with Carmelo Anthony emerged as one of the era's most intriguing dynamics, a union of two prolific scorers whose styles promised fireworks. At 22, Melo was the budding franchise face, averaging 28.9 points in 2006-07, while Iverson brought veteran savvy and relentless drive. Their first game together, after Melo's suspension, saw them combine for 51 points in a win, igniting visions of an unstoppable tandem. On court, it was explosive: Iverson's quickness complemented Melo's mid-range lethality, creating mismatches that defenses struggled to contain. Yet complications arose from overlapping roles, both alpha personalities vying for touches in a ball-dominant era. Iverson later admitted the experiment faltered due to youth and inexperience, not ego clashes. Offensively, their net rating soared in pick-and-roll sets, but defensive lapses—allowing opponents higher efficiency—exposed vulnerabilities. Emotionally, the partnership fostered mutual respect; Iverson praised Melo's work ethic, while Melo absorbed lessons in leadership. It was a complicated ballet of talent and temperament, where brilliance clashed with inefficiency. Culturally, their duo amplified Iverson's influence, blending hip-hop flair with Melo's street credibility, drawing diverse crowds to Pepsi Center. This alliance, though brief, reshaped perceptions of superstar pairings, foreshadowing future experiments in the league's star-driven landscape.

The Iverson-Melo tandem's cultural ripple extended beyond stats, injecting a raw, urban energy into Denver's basketball scene. Two icons of Black culture—Iverson with his tattoos and defiance, Melo with his Baltimore grit—created a synergy that transcended the game. Fans noted increased diversity in arenas, with more women and hip-hop enthusiasts attending, drawn by the duo's charisma and style. Iverson's influence on fashion and attitude amplified Melo's early career, as the younger star adopted elements of AI's unapologetic persona. Analytically, their presence boosted merchandise sales and national TV appearances, putting the Nuggets on the map in a league dominated by coastal powers. Emotionally, it represented a bridge between generations: Iverson's '90s rebellion meeting Melo's millennial polish. Critics debated if this cultural fusion distracted from winning, but it undeniably broadened the NBA's appeal, challenging stereotypes and embracing authenticity. In Denver, their partnership symbolized resilience amid scrutiny, as Iverson navigated being a co-headliner. This era highlighted how players like them reshaped fan engagement, blending sport with cultural expression. Yet, underlying tensions—defensive shortcomings and playoff exits—hinted at limitations, forcing Iverson to confront evolving team dynamics. The pairing's legacy lies in its vibrancy, a testament to how individual flair could ignite collective passion, even if championships eluded them.

Denver offered Iverson a canvas for a subtler form of leadership, one less about singular dominance and more about collective elevation. No longer the sole focal point, he embraced mentoring roles, sharing insights from his MVP days with Melo and others. His voice in huddles carried weight, urging accountability in a young locker room. Analytically, this shift coincided with career-high assists, peaking at 7.2 per game, as he adapted to facilitating alongside scorers. Emotionally, it was liberating yet humbling—free from Philly's burdens but stripped of absolute control. Iverson's charisma fostered unity, his stories of adversity inspiring resilience. Culturally, this phase reinforced his role as a trailblazer, guiding the next wave in navigating fame's pitfalls. Yet, off-court habits lingered, drawing criticism amid the team's inconsistent defense. The Nuggets' 50-win season in 2007-08 showcased potential, but first-round losses underscored the need for balance. Iverson's leadership here was introspective, blending fiery motivation with quiet wisdom, a departure from his earlier bravado. It revealed a maturing athlete, one learning that influence extended beyond points. In this environment, he tapped into empathy, understanding teammates' struggles as mirrors of his own. Denver thus became a turning point, where leadership evolved from command to collaboration, preparing him for the uncertainties ahead.

On-court brilliance punctuated Iverson's Denver tenure, interspersed with the realities of off-court recalibration. Games like his 44-point explosion against the Lakers reminded the league of his undiminished quickness, crossovers still dismantling defenses. Teaming with Melo, they orchestrated scoring barrages, like a combined 70 points in wins that electrified crowds. Analytically, Iverson's efficiency dipped slightly, but his usage rate highlighted his pivotal role.

Emotionally, these peaks provided solace amid adjustment pains—new routines, media scrutiny, and the altitude's physical toll. Off court, he balanced family life with Denver's nightlife, his tattoos a constant amid change. Culturally aware observers noted how his presence invigorated the city's hip-hop scene, blending with Melo's aura. Yet, injuries crept in, forcing missed games and reflections on mortality. The league's shift toward analytics questioned his iso-heavy style, but Iverson's heart-driven play endured. These moments of glory, like buzzer-beaters and All-Star nods, affirmed his greatness, even as wear accumulated. Balancing brilliance with adaptation, Denver tested his adaptability, revealing a player still capable of magic but increasingly aware of limits. It was a chapter of highs tempered by realism, where on-court fire met off-court introspection, shaping a more nuanced legacy.

As Iverson settled in Denver, the NBA itself was morphing into a new era, with styles and stars signaling a departure from his isolation-driven heyday. The mid-2000s saw the rise of versatile forwards like LeBron James and Kevin Durant, emphasizing efficiency and team play over individual heroics. Analytics gained traction, prioritizing three-pointers and pace, areas where Iverson's game, rooted in mid-range artistry, faced scrutiny. Emotionally, this evolution stirred a sense of displacement for Iverson, a pioneer now viewed as a relic in a league chasing championships through balance. Kobe Bryant's Lakers and Tim Duncan's Spurs exemplified disciplined success, contrasting the Nuggets' flashy but flawed approach. Culturally, the influx of international talent diversified rosters, diluting the hip-hop dominance Iverson embodied. Yet, his influence persisted, inspiring guards like Derrick Rose to blend speed with scoring. Analytically, league-wide scoring dipped post-hand-check rules, but Iverson adapted, maintaining high outputs. This period forced him to confront shifting expectations, where MVPs were measured by rings as much as stats. The transition highlighted generational tensions, with Iverson's defiance clashing against emerging narratives of sustainability. In this evolving landscape, he navigated with grit, his style a bridge between eras, even as the game accelerated beyond his prime.

Age and accumulated wear began to etch lines on Iverson's once-invincible frame, compelling a navigation through diminished expectations and physical tolls. Turning 32 in Denver, he battled ankle sprains and knee issues, missing games that once seemed inconceivable for the ironman. Analytically, his scoring held at 26.4 points in 2007-08, but efficiency waned, with shooting percentages dipping amid heavier defensive schemes. Emotionally, this phase evoked frustration and reflection; no longer the boundless force, Iverson grappled with mortality, his explosive first step occasionally betraying him. Critics pointed to his practice habits—or lack thereof—as culprits, but Iverson viewed them as part of his unique rhythm. Culturally, his perseverance resonated with fans who saw in him the human side of stardom, a Black athlete defying odds in a scrutinizing world. Shifting league expectations demanded more from veterans: leadership without the ball, defense in schemes. Iverson adapted unevenly, his passion undimmed but body protesting. Moments of doubt surfaced, yet his resilience shone, drawing on Virginia roots for strength. This era tested his identity, blending analytical decline with emotional fortitude, as he learned to value impact beyond numbers. In Denver's thin air, he confronted the inevitable, emerging wiser, if wearier, in a career's twilight.

Critics and analysts, once polarized by Iverson's flash, began reassessing his place as his career arced downward. Early detractors decried his inefficiency and team impact, but late-career views softened, acknowledging his cultural revolution and scoring prowess. Publications like ESPN highlighted how he normalized Black expression in the NBA, from attire to attitude, influencing a generation. Analytically, advanced metrics revealed his offensive gravity, drawing doubles that opened lanes for others, even if wins were sparse. Emotionally, this reevaluation offered validation amid criticism; Iverson's authenticity, once maligned, now celebrated as trailblazing. Figures like Shaquille O'Neal praised his realness, while younger players cited him as inspiration. Yet, some persisted in labeling him a non-winner, pointing to playoff shortcomings. In Denver, his role sparked debates on superstar pairings' viability. Culturally aware analyses positioned him as a bridge to modern stars, his defiance paving paths for tattoos and personal brands. This period's discourse blended nostalgia with critique, humanizing Iverson beyond stats. He reflected on regrets, like not heeding Larry Brown's advice on game study, showing self-awareness. Ultimately, reassessments affirmed his Hall of Fame worth, a complex figure whose impact transcended rings, reshaping how greatness was measured.

Scattered moments of brilliance pierced the narrative of decline, reminding fans why Iverson remained an enigma of greatness. In Denver, a 51-point masterpiece against the Clippers showcased vintage crossovers and pull-ups, his slight frame defying logic. Later, in limited action, he dropped 30-plus outbursts that evoked Philly's glory days. Analytically, these peaks maintained his All-Star status, with steals and assists underscoring versatility. Emotionally, they fueled a fire against doubters, proving his heart outpaced his years. Culturally, such displays reinforced his icon status, clips circulating in hip-hop montages. Against the Lakers or Spurs, his duels with Kobe or Parker harkened to rivalries past, blending nostalgia with intensity. Yet, these flashes coexisted with inconsistency, injuries curtailing sustained runs. In Detroit, a rare 38-point game hinted at potential, but context dimmed its shine. Memphis offered fewer highlights, but his brief tenacity inspired. These instances, like dunks that didn't count or clutch threes, affirmed his brilliance amid fade. They served as emotional anchors, for Iverson and fans, preserving the myth of invincibility. In a league favoring youth, his sparks illuminated enduring talent, a testament to willpower over wear.

The emotional weight of no longer being "the franchise" settled heavily on Iverson, a profound shift from Philly's singular devotion. In Denver, sharing billing with Melo meant ceding the narrative, his shots distributed, his aura shared. On one hand, this democratized offense boosted team efficiency but diluted his individual spotlight. Emotionally, it evoked isolation; accustomed to carrying burdens, he now navigated ensemble dynamics, his ego tested by secondary roles. Culturally, this humbled a symbol of defiance, forcing introspection on legacy beyond stardom. Whispers of trade value stung, reminding him of expendability. Yet, it fostered growth, appreciating collaboration's joys amid losses. No longer the savior, he relished moments of support, like Melo's encouragement. This phase stripped illusions, revealing vulnerability beneath bravado. Fans sensed the melancholy, his post-game demeanor quieter, reflective. In a career defined by independence, this demotion challenged his core, blending resentment with acceptance. It underscored the NBA's cruelty, where icons become pieces in puzzles. Iverson's response—persistent effort—highlighted resilience, but the ache lingered, a quiet lament for lost centrality.

The move from Denver came abruptly on November 3, 2008, traded to the Detroit Pistons for Chauncey Billups, Antonio McDyess, and Cheikh Samb—a deal that prioritized championship pedigree over Iverson's flair. In Motor City, he averaged a career-low 17.4 points, clashing with coach Michael Curry's system that benched him at times. Emotionally, the demotion to sixth man role ignited frustration, leading to missed practices and public discord. Analytically, his efficiency suffered amid role ambiguity, the Pistons missing playoffs for the first time in years. Culturally, Detroit's blue-collar ethos clashed with Iverson's individualism, amplifying isolation. Brief stints of scoring offered glimpses, but injuries and discontent dominated. Then, in September 2009, he signed with Memphis on a one-year deal, hoping for revival, but lasted just three games, averaging 12.3 points off the bench. Disagreements over starting status led to his release, a nadir that exposed vulnerabilities. These transitions, from contender to also-ran, forced harsh realities: age, 34 by Memphis, and league shifts left him adrift. Yet, they seeded reinvention, as Iverson pondered life beyond stardom.

In Detroit and Memphis, Iverson confronted humility's harsh lessons, stripping away the armor of invincibility. Bench roles and short leashes humbled a former MVP, teaching patience amid ego bruises. Emotionally, these lows—courtroom battles over personal matters, ignored by teams—prompted self-reevaluation, as he later admitted hitting rock bottom. Analytically, reduced minutes highlighted decline, but his tenacity in sparse appearances showcased enduring spirit. Culturally, this phase humanized him, a Black icon navigating prejudice and fading relevance with grace. Resilience emerged in quiet ways: accepting lesser contracts, reflecting on regrets like not studying film more. Reinvention meant embracing vulnerability, turning pain into wisdom for others.

These years, though brief and bittersweet, forged a deeper character, blending defiance with acceptance. Iverson learned that legacy endured through influence, not just accolades. As opportunities dwindled, his journey underscored perseverance's power, setting the stage for one final, poignant chapter.

The wanderings through Detroit and Memphis left Iverson at a crossroads, his career a mosaic of triumph and trial. Free agency loomed in 2009, with calls from teams scarce, forcing contemplation of retirement or overseas play. Emotionally, the silence stung, a far cry from the adulation of youth. Yet, whispers of a return to Philadelphia began circulating, a potential homecoming that promised closure and celebration. Analysts speculated on the fit, a veteran guard in a rebuilding squad, but the cultural pull was undeniable—back to the city that birthed his legend. Iverson's heart, ever tied to Philly's streets, yearned for redemption, a chance to rewrite the farewell. This setup evoked anticipation, blending nostalgia with hope, as the prodigal son eyed the horizon.

Detroit, Memphis & Return to Philly

By the fall of 2008, Allen Iverson's time in Denver had unraveled like a frayed jersey, threads pulling apart under the weight of unmet expectations. The Nuggets, once invigorated by his arrival, had plateaued in the playoffs, their high-octane offense clashing with defensive lapses that Iverson's style couldn't fully mask. Traded to the Detroit Pistons in a deal that sent Chauncey Billups the other way, Iverson stepped into uncertainty, his career at a crossroads where stardom met obsolescence. At 33, he was no longer the untouchable force who'd redefined guard play, but a veteran whose explosive drives and crossover wizardry now carried the asterisk of age and inefficiency. The trade stung—not just for leaving a contending team, but for the implicit message: Denver sought stability over spectacle. Iverson arrived in Motor City amid whispers of revival, yet the fit felt off from the jump, a cultural mismatch in a franchise still echoing its gritty, championship ethos from the mid-2000s. Detroit's fans, hardened by economic downturns mirroring the city's own struggles, hoped Iverson's fire could reignite a fading contender. But beneath the surface, doubts simmered. Iverson's individualism, once revolutionary, now clashed with the NBA's shifting tides toward analytics-driven team play. His emotional armor, forged in Philadelphia's adoring chaos, began to crack as he pondered his diminishing role, the uncertainty gnawing at a pride that had always been his greatest ally and foe.

From the outset, the Detroit experiment was a collision of worlds, Iverson's freewheeling artistry grinding against the Pistons' disciplined machinery. Traded on November 3, 2008, he debuted with 24 points, but the integration was rocky. Coach Michael Curry envisioned him as a scoring punch off the bench, a role Iverson viewed as an insult to his legacy. Friction built quickly; Iverson started the first 54 games he played, averaging 17.4 points, yet the team's chemistry faltered. Detroit, built on the Bad Boys' legacy of collective toughness, symbolized the league's evolution away from solo heroes toward ensemble casts. Iverson's iso-heavy game, brilliant in isolation, disrupted the flow that had defined the Pistons' success. Off-court, cultural divides deepened—Detroit's blue-collar ethos clashed with Iverson's hip-hop-infused persona, his cornrows and tattoos a reminder of the cultural shift he'd pioneered but now seemed out of step with the NBA's polished image. The emotional toll was palpable; Iverson, who'd always played with a chip on his shoulder, felt the weight of being traded for a point guard known for steadiness over flash. It was as if the league was signaling that heart and hustle alone weren't enough anymore. Critics pointed to his shooting percentages—around 41 percent in Detroit—as evidence of decline, while fans still chanted his name, a bittersweet chorus underscoring his enduring appeal amid growing irrelevance.

The tension escalated into outright conflict, fracturing Iverson's stint in Detroit beyond repair. By March 2009, after a back injury sidelined him, the Pistons announced he'd sit out the season's remainder, a decision Iverson publicly decried as a benching in disguise. "I'm not a reserve," he stated flatly in interviews, his voice laced with the pain of demotion. The organization, under GM Joe Dumars, prioritized youth and structure, viewing Iverson as a disruptive force rather than a savior. This symbolized broader NBA changes: the rise of efficiency metrics, where Iverson's volume scoring gave way to players like LeBron James, who balanced individualism with facilitation. Iverson's frustration boiled over in private workouts and public statements, his pride clashing with the reality of no longer being the alpha. Emotionally, it was devastating—the man who'd carried franchises on his slender frame now felt expendable, a franchise cornerstone reduced to trade bait. Detroit's fans, loyal yet pragmatic, watched with mixed feelings; some adored his tenacity, others lamented the lost cohesion. Iverson's internal battles raged: the fighter from Hampton who defied odds now grappled with obsolescence, his heart-heavy introspection revealing a vulnerability rarely shown. The city's own decline mirrored his—once dominant, now rebuilding—amplifying the bittersweet narrative of a star fading against a changing backdrop.

As free agency loomed in the summer of 2009, Iverson's options narrowed, his market value diminished by the Detroit debacle. Teams hesitated, wary of his demands for starter minutes amid his age and injury history. The

Memphis Grizzlies emerged as a suitor, signing him to a one-year deal on September 10, 2009, with promises of opportunity. Yet, this chapter was doomed from the start, a short-lived experiment that collapsed under mismatched expectations. Iverson arrived envisioning a starring role, but coach Lionel Hollins slotted him as a sixth man behind Mike Conley. The Grizzlies, a young squad building around Rudy Gay and Zach Randolph, sought grit without disruption. Iverson's pride recoiled; after just three games—averaging 12.3 points off the bench—he left the team on November 7, citing personal reasons but fueled by frustration over his role. The emotional undercurrents were profound: Iverson, who'd reshaped basketball culture with his unapologetic authenticity, now faced a league prizing adaptability over iconoclasm. Memphis symbolized the NBA's pivot to analytics and youth, where Iverson's improvisational genius felt archaic. Fans across the league still revered him, packing arenas for glimpses of The Answer, but critics wrote him off as a relic, his pain manifesting in withdrawn silences and defiant interviews.

The Memphis implosion laid bare Iverson's internal turmoil, a storm of pain, pride, and unresolved battles. At 34, he confronted the erosion of his identity as basketball's cultural vanguard. The pride that propelled him from poverty to stardom now isolated him, refusing compromises that lesser players accepted. Emotionally, it was a gut punch—the adulation from fans, who mobbed him in streets and stadiums, contrasted sharply with executives' cold calculations. Iverson's introspection deepened; friends noted his quieter demeanor, the fire dimmed by repeated rejections. This period encapsulated the NBA's evolution: the emergence of superteams and efficiency kings like Kobe Bryant in his twilight or the budding dominance of Kevin Durant. Iverson's style, once the blueprint for guards like Russell Westbrook, now seemed inefficient in a pace-and-space era. Critics lambasted his unwillingness to evolve, labeling him stubborn, while supporters saw it as principled defiance. The bittersweet irony was stark— the man who'd normalized tattoos and cornrows in the league now felt alienated by its corporate sheen. His pain wasn't just professional; it was existential, questioning a life's worth tied to a game that had moved on.

Amid the wreckage, glimmers of loyalty persisted, fans' unwavering love a salve against the critics' dismissals. Social media buzzed with tributes, old highlights recirculating like digital relics, reminding Iverson of his indelible mark. Yet, the league's new era loomed, with stars like Derrick Rose embodying explosive athleticism tempered by team-first mentalities. Iverson's frustration with role changes peaked; he'd always been the engine, not the accessory. The emotional impact of no longer being a cornerstone was crushing—nights spent reflecting on Philly's glory days, where he was beloved despite flaws. Detroit and Memphis had stripped that away, leaving scars of doubt. As offers dwindled, Iverson's path veered toward reconciliation, whispers of a Philadelphia return gaining traction. The Sixers, mired in mediocrity, saw value in his veteran presence and box-office draw. For Iverson, it was more than basketball; it was a homecoming laced with nostalgia, a chance to reclaim dignity in the city that defined him.

Negotiations crystallized in December 2009, the Philadelphia 76ers signing Iverson to a non-guaranteed deal on December 2. The announcement sent ripples through the league, a poignant full-circle moment for a prodigal son. Stepping back into the Wells Fargo Center, Iverson was greeted by thunderous applause, tears streaming down his face during his debut on December 7 against Denver. Averaging 13.9 points in 25 games, his play was a shadow of peak form, but the emotional resonance was profound. For Iverson, it represented redemption and closure, the city's embrace, healing wounds from trades and tribulations. Philadelphia, with its underdog spirit, mirrored his own—resilient, flawed, unbreakable. Fans packed seats, chanting "MVP" in echoes of 2001, a bittersweet reminder of lost youth. Culturally, it underscored Iverson's lasting impact: the tattoos, the attitude, now mainstream, yet his return highlighted the NBA's generational shift. Emotionally, he battled pride against acceptance, knowing this might be the end.

Iverson's final months as a Sixer unfolded like a slow fade, each game a meditation on legacy and loss. Injuries mounted—a calf strain, arthritis in his knee—forcing him to miss time, including a poignant absence for his daughter's health issues. On February 22, 2010, he played his last NBA game, scoring 13 points in a loss to the Spurs, unaware it was farewell. The organization parted ways in March, citing personal reasons, but the subtext was clear: Iverson's era was closing. The emotional weight was immense—for him, a quiet reckoning with mortality in a sport that devours its icons; for the city, a collective sigh over a hero's twilight. Philadelphia had always seen Iverson as family, flaws and all, his return a cathartic bridge between past glory and uncertain future. Bittersweet hues colored every moment: the standing ovations, the jersey sales, juxtaposed with empty stats lines. It represented the end of an archetype—the undersized warrior who bent the game to his will—yielding to a new breed.

Yet, in those final echoes, Iverson's influence lingered, setting the stage for his cultural afterlife. The NBA he'd reshaped continued evolving, but his imprint on style, resilience, and authenticity endured beyond the court. As he stepped away, the sense of an era closing was palpable, a door shutting on the raw, unfiltered passion that defined him.

In the quiet aftermath, Iverson reflected on the journey—from Detroit's discord to Memphis's brevity, back to Philly's embrace. The pain of diminished roles had forged a deeper introspection, his pride tempered by time's inexorable march. Fans' love remained a constant, a testament to his transcendence, even as critics consigned him to history. The league's new stars carried fragments of his DNA, but the original mold was breaking. Returning home offered solace, a poignant bookend to a career that defied norms.

The homecoming's meaning deepened with each passing day, for Iverson and Philadelphia alike. It was a mutual healing— the city reclaiming its icon, him rediscovering his roots amid upheaval. Emotionally, it mended fractures from years of wandering, affirming that legacy isn't just stats but the hearts touched. His final moments as a Sixer symbolized closure, a bittersweet farewell to the hardwood battles that shaped him.

As the cheers faded, Iverson stood at the threshold of what came next, his cultural resonance poised to echo far beyond retirement. The era of The Answer was closing, but its questions lingered, challenging the game he'd forever changed.

The path back to Philadelphia had been circuitous, paved with rejections that tested Iverson's resolve. Yet, in signing that December contract, he found a measure of peace, the city's fervor a balm for bruised ego. His play, though limited, reignited sparks of old magic—crossovers that drew gasps, drives that evoked memories. Emotionally, it was restorative, affirming his worth in a place that never doubted.

Critics continued their obituaries, but fans' devotion drowned them out, a chorus of loyalty in a changing NBA. The league's evolution—toward three-point barrages and positional fluidity—highlighted Iverson's pioneering role, even as it rendered him an anachronism. His internal battles subsided in Philly's warmth, pride yielding to gratitude.

Those last games carried symbolic weight, each possession a nod to perseverance. Iverson's exit, quiet and unceremonious, represented the end of an individualistic epoch, making way for collaborative dynasties. For Philadelphia, it was a shared mourning, the city's son bidding adieu.

In retrospect, Detroit and Memphis were necessary detours, forging the humility that sweetened his return. The emotional arc—frustration to fulfillment—underscored his humanity, a star grappling with twilight. As the curtain fell, Iverson's cultural afterlife beckoned, his influence immortalized in the game's fabric.

The chapter's close found Iverson in Philadelphia, the sense of finality heavy yet hopeful. His journey's scars had deepened his legend, setting the stage for legacies that transcend wins and losses. An era was indeed closing, but Iverson's light, though dimmed, would never fully extinguish.

The Final Chapters

As the calendar flipped into the late 2000s, Allen Iverson's once-unstoppable drive on the court began to encounter the unyielding barriers of time, injury, and shifting team dynamics. After a trade from the Denver Nuggets to the Detroit Pistons in November 2008, Iverson found himself in a new ecosystem, one that didn't revolve around his scoring prowess or improvisational genius. He appeared in 54 games that season, averaging 17.4 points and 4.9 assists, but the Pistons' rigid structure clashed with his free-flowing style. Starting roles gave way to bench minutes, a demotion that stung deeply for a player who had always been the alpha. By April 2009, a back injury sidelined him for the playoffs, and Iverson publicly mused about retirement rather than accepting a reduced role. It was a harbinger of the internal conflict brewing—the man who had redefined guard play now grappling with a league that seemed to be moving on without him. That summer, he signed a one-year deal with the Memphis Grizzlies, hoping for a starter's spot, but after just three games and 13.3 points per outing, personal frustrations boiled over. He left the team citing family matters, his contract terminated mutually in November 2009. These brief stints weren't just professional footnotes; they exposed the raw vulnerability of a legend facing obsolescence, his body betraying the heart that still burned for the game. In Philadelphia, where his myth was born, fans watched with a mix of hope and heartache, knowing the Answer's questions were growing more profound.

The return to Philadelphia in December 2009 felt like a homecoming scripted from the city's gritty soul. Signing a non-guaranteed minimum contract with the 76ers, Iverson stepped onto the Wells Fargo Center floor to a thunderous ovation, the kind that echoed the unbreakable bond between player and place. In his debut, he scored 11 points with six assists, but it was the energy—the palpable electricity—that reminded everyone of his transformative era. Over 25 games, he averaged 13.9 points, flashing remnants of the crossover that had humiliated defenders league-wide. He even earned an 11th All-Star nod, a testament to his enduring popularity. Yet, beneath the surface, turmoil simmered. In February 2010, Iverson departed indefinitely to tend to his daughter Messiah's illness, later revealed as Kawasaki disease, a condition that demanded his full attention as a father. His final NBA appearance came against the Chicago Bulls, a quiet 13-point effort in a loss that symbolized the anticlimactic fade. This wasn't the triumphant exit fans envisioned; it was a poignant interruption, forcing Iverson to confront priorities beyond basketball. The struggle wasn't merely physical—aches from years of fearless drives—but emotional, as the game that had been his salvation now slipped away. In interviews later, he reflected on being "mentally absent" during those last games, his mind fractured by personal crises. Philadelphia's embrace offered solace, but it couldn't mask the void opening within him, a cultural icon wrestling with the silence after the roar.

Venturing overseas marked Iverson's desperate bid to reclaim the thrill that the NBA no longer provided. In October 2010, he inked a two-year, $4 million deal with Beşiktaş in Turkey, drawn by the promise of stardom in the Turkish Basketball Super League and EuroCup. His debut brought 15 points in a EuroCup loss, and over 10 games, he averaged 14.3 points domestically and 11.5 in Europe. Fans in Istanbul treated him like royalty, a reminder of his global appeal, but the physical toll was unrelenting. A calf injury forced his return to the U.S. in January 2011 for surgery, effectively ending his stint abroad. Brief flirtations with other leagues followed—rumors of play in Lithuania or Latvia—but nothing materialized into sustained action. These short stops weren't triumphant conquests; they were echoes of a career in twilight, Iverson chasing the adrenaline that had defined him since Georgetown. The cultural dissonance added layers: a Hampton, Virginia, kid navigating foreign courts, his braids and tattoos standing out amid new crowds. Back home, media narratives painted him as a faded star unwilling to let go, but those close to him saw a deeper fight—a refusal to surrender the identity basketball had forged. This period crystallized his struggle, the Answer searching for questions in unfamiliar arenas, only to find that the game's pull couldn't heal the accumulating scars of transition.

By October 2013, Iverson stood before the Philadelphia faithful to formally announce his retirement, a moment heavy with reflection and release. "I just don't have the desire to play anymore," he admitted, his words carrying the weight of a decade's battles. The ceremony at the 76ers' home opener drew standing ovations, a collective exhale from a city that had witnessed his peaks and valleys. Yet, the path to this point had been fraught: financial rumors swirled, personal life upheavals like his 2010 divorce from Tawanna loomed, and the emotional drain of his daughter's health crisis lingered. Iverson's struggle with closure wasn't theatrical; it was profoundly human, a man who had poured his soul into every possession now facing an empty court. In quieter moments, he grappled with the mental fog of those final seasons, admitting to being "absent" amid family strife. Retirement didn't come as liberation but as a reluctant acceptance, the fire that fueled 30-point nights dimming to embers. Culturally, this marked a pivot: no longer the defiant underdog, Iverson began to embody resilience in repose. Fans sensed the shift, their cheers laced with nostalgia for the era he defined. As he stepped away, the NBA's landscape—now dotted with players echoing his flair—served as a living testament to his indelible mark, even as he navigated the unfamiliar terrain of life without the ball.

In the years immediately following his retirement, Iverson's public image evolved from the rebellious firebrand to a more introspective figure, one weary of defending his narrative but resolute in his authenticity. No longer bound by game schedules, he surfaced in endorsements and appearances, like his 2014 jersey retirement ceremony in Philadelphia, where legends gathered to honor him. Rumors of financial woes—debunked by Iverson himself as myths—persisted, but he focused on reclaiming his story, emphasizing no regrets about his path. "I wouldn't change anything," he once said, reflecting on the tattoos, the cornrows, the unfiltered press conferences that had drawn both adoration and scrutiny. Media outlets began softening their lenses, portraying him not as a cautionary tale but as a pioneer who humanized superstars. His involvement in the BIG3 league starting in 2017, as player-coach for 3's Company, offered glimpses of the old magic—limited minutes yielding flashes of crossovers—but it was more about legacy than conquest. Culturally grounded in his Hampton roots, Iverson remained tied to hip-hop circles, collaborating on projects that bridged his worlds. This phase revealed a man at peace with his imperfections, his public persona shifting from defiant to dignified, a cultural touchstone whose influence quietly permeated without the need for constant validation. Fans connected to this vulnerability, seeing in him the emotional arc of their own journeys.

The seeds of Iverson's cultural immortality sprouted subtly in those early post-playing days, as his imprint on basketball's ethos began to crystallize beyond statistics. No longer confined to highlight reels, his essence—raw, unapologetic expression—resonated in broader conversations about identity and authenticity. Fashion houses nodded to his style, with throwback jerseys and durags reemerging in streetwear lines, while music artists like Post Malone immortalized him in tracks like "White Iverson," blending his swagger with contemporary beats. This wasn't mere nostalgia; it was the dawning recognition of how Iverson had mainstreamed elements of Black urban culture into the NBA's mainstream. Younger generations, scrolling through social media, discovered his 2001 Finals heroics or the infamous practice rant, reframing them as acts of rebellion against conformity. In Philadelphia, murals and tributes popped up, embedding him in the city's fabric. His retirement didn't dim his aura; it amplified it, allowing space for reflection on how one 6-foot guard had shifted the league's cultural axis. Emotionally, this immortality brought a quiet validation, a counter to the struggles of his final years. As media retrospectives multiplied, Iverson's story transformed from controversial to canonical, a narrative of triumph over adversity that invited deeper cultural grounding.

Younger players in the NBA carried Iverson's torch forward, their games infused with echoes of his fearless innovation and stylistic flair. Kyrie Irving's lethal handles and creative finishes bore the mark of Iverson's crossover, a move that had revolutionized guard play. Russell Westbrook's relentless drives and emotional intensity mirrored the Answer's all-out ethos, while Ja Morant's acrobatic fearlessness evoked Iverson's refusal to back down from bigger foes. Even Stephen Curry, with his perimeter wizardry, acknowledged Iverson's role in empowering smaller players to dominate. "He showed us how to be ourselves," players like these often noted, crediting Iverson for normalizing tattoos, braids, and personal expression on the court. In interviews, emerging stars spoke of studying his tapes, not just for technique but for the cultural confidence he exuded. This influence wasn't superficial; it was generational, passing through locker rooms where Iverson's jerseys hung as talismans. As the league evolved into a more player-empowered era, his blueprint became evident in contract negotiations and off-court ventures. Emotionally, this continuity offered Iverson a sense of purpose in retirement, watching from afar as his struggles paved the way for others' freedoms. Culturally, it grounded basketball in authenticity, ensuring his legacy lived through the next wave's triumphs.

Fans forged a profound, nostalgic bond with Iverson in his post-playing era, their connection deepening into something almost spiritual. In arenas across the league, spontaneous ovations greeted his appearances, like at the 2016 All-Star Game or the NBA's 75th Anniversary celebration, where cheers swelled for the man who had embodied underdog grit. Social media amplified this, with viral clips of his step-over on Tyronn Lue or 48-point Finals outburst evoking collective memories of an era when basketball felt more personal, more raw. For Black fans especially, Iverson represented unfiltered pride, his journey from Hampton's streets to stardom mirroring their own aspirations and hurdles. Emotional tributes poured in—letters, murals, fan art—capturing the heartache of his career's end while celebrating its highs. In Philadelphia, this nostalgia manifested in sold-out jersey nights and chants of "A.I." that lingered long after games. It wasn't just about wins; it was the cultural resonance, the way he made fans feel seen in his defiance. As years passed, this connection evolved from admiration to reverence, an emotional lifeline for those who saw in Iverson's vulnerabilities their own. His stepping back allowed space for this myth-making, fans filling the void with stories that immortalized him as more than a player—a symbol of resilience.

A new wave of media scrutiny reevaluated Iverson's career, shifting from criticism to nuanced appreciation of his complexities. Outlets like ESPN and The Ringer delved into the context behind his infamous 2002 practice rant, revealing it unfolded amid grief over his best friend Rahsaan Langeford's murder and team frustrations. What once seemed like petulance was recast as raw vulnerability, Iverson's repetition of "practice" a defense against deeper pains. Documentaries and biographies, such as the 2014 film "Iverson" and Kent Babb's 2015 book "Not a Game," unpacked his off-court struggles—probation, family losses, media biases—framing them as integral to his triumph. This reevaluation highlighted how Iverson challenged the NBA's polished image, paving the way for today's expressive athletes. Culturally grounded pieces explored his role in blending hip-hop with hoops, crediting him for diversifying the league's narrative. Emotionally, this shift brought vindication, countering years of narratives that painted him as problematic. As podcasts and long-form articles proliferated, Iverson's story gained layers, from MVP glory to retirement reflections, fostering a more empathetic understanding. This media pivot not only redeemed his image but amplified his cultural immortality, setting the stage for broader recognition.

Iverson gradually receded from the daily spotlight, choosing a life of selective visibility that balanced privacy with presence. No longer chasing headlines, he surfaced at key events—BIG3 games, All-Star weekends, endorsement launches—where his mere appearance sparked waves of applause. Partnerships with Reebok and Viola Brands kept him connected to his roots in fashion and culture, while collaborations like the TikTok ad with Tyronn Lue added playful nods to his past. In 2023, he rejoined Reebok as Vice President of Basketball alongside Shaquille O'Neal, a role that allowed him to shape the brand that had defined his sneaker legacy. Yet, this wasn't a full-throated return; it was measured, reflective of a man who had learned to savor moments amid losses like those of mentors John Thompson and Kobe Bryant. Emotionally, stepping back provided space for healing, away from the relentless scrutiny that had marked his playing days. Culturally, his presence remained potent—social media shoutouts and music references ensured he stayed relevant without overexposure. In Philadelphia, he was a quiet fixture, attending games and community events, his bond with the city undiminished. This era of restraint highlighted his growth, a cultural icon content to let his influence echo rather than shout.

Iverson's relationship with Philadelphia deepened into an enduring romance after retirement, the city embracing him as its eternal son. The 2014 retirement of his No. 3 jersey drew tears and cheers, legends like Julius Erving toasting his impact. In 2024, the 76ers unveiled a statue outside their practice facility, capturing his crossover in bronze—a symbol of Philly's gritty soul immortalized. "Our bond is unique," Iverson often reflected, crediting the fans' tough love for forging his resilience. He returned for alumni nights and charity events, his ovations rivaling those for current stars. This connection wasn't one-sided; Iverson professed undying love for the city that drafted him in 1996, crediting it for his identity. Amid personal lows, Philly's support offered emotional anchor, countering isolation. Culturally, it grounded his legacy in the streets where hip-hop blared and underdogs dreamed. Fans saw in him their struggles—poverty, prejudice—mirrored in his rise. As the Sixers chased championships, Iverson's presence reminded them of past glories, his statue a beacon for future generations. This post-retirement harmony healed old wounds from trade tensions, solidifying Philadelphia as the heart of his story.

Emerging themes in Iverson's cultural legacy wove together fashion, music, and identity, painting him as a bridge between streets and stardom. His cornrows and tattoos, once league taboos, became emblems of Black expression, influencing designers who incorporated durags and chains into high fashion. Reebok's A.I. line persisted, with retro releases evoking his era's swagger. In music, his hip-hop ties—freestyling in clubs, endorsements from artists like Jadakiss—fused with basketball, inspiring tracks that sampled his press conferences. Post Malone's "White Iverson" hit billions of streams, blending his name with trap beats, a testament to his crossover appeal. Identity-wise, Iverson embodied unapologetic authenticity, challenging norms of athlete decorum and empowering marginalized voices. This legacy wasn't static; it evolved in social media threads where young creators dissected his impact on self-expression. Emotionally, these themes provided validation, turning past criticisms into celebrations. Culturally grounded in Hampton's rhythms, his story resonated with those navigating dual worlds. As retrospectives mounted, these elements coalesced, framing Iverson not just as a player but a cultural architect whose influence rippled through generations.

The growing understanding of Iverson's impact on athlete expression revealed how he dismantled barriers, allowing players to embrace their full selves. Tattoos, once hidden, became badges of honor post-Iverson, with stars like LeBron James crediting him for normalizing body art as storytelling. His refusal to conform—wearing baggy jeans and durags amid dress code crackdowns—sparked a league-wide shift toward individuality. "He made it okay to be you," echoed in player testimonials, highlighting how his authenticity countered the NBA's corporate polish. This expression extended to mental health discussions; Iverson's candidness about grief and struggles paved paths for modern athletes to speak openly. Culturally, it grounded basketball in real-world identities, blending hip-hop's bravado with on-court artistry. Emotionally, this recognition healed old scars, reframing his "rebellious" image as revolutionary. Younger players adopted his flair—braids, jewelry—transforming tunnels into runways. As media reevaluated, his role in empowering Black athletes gained prominence, a legacy of liberation. This understanding deepened in retirement, positioning Iverson as a forefather of the player-empowered era.

Whispers of Hall of Fame recognition began stirring even before Iverson's 2013 retirement announcement, as analysts debated his eligibility amid his transformative stats and cultural footprint. His 2001 MVP, four scoring titles, and 26,000-plus points made a compelling case, but it was the intangible influence—shifting the guard archetype—that sowed the seeds. In 2014, his jersey retirement hinted at broader honors, with NBA insiders predicting induction. Iverson himself downplayed it, focusing on family and reflection, yet the anticipation built emotional momentum. Media pieces positioned him alongside Shaquille O'Neal and Yao Ming, emphasizing his underdog narrative. This period marked a preparatory phase, where his career's highs were cataloged against lows, fostering appreciation. Culturally, it grounded his story in resilience, a Hampton kid eyed for immortality. Fans rallied online, petitions and tributes amplifying the call. As

2016 approached, these seeds blossomed into certainty, setting the stage for canonization.

Iverson's emergence as a cultural elder unfolded organically, his wisdom dispensed through interviews and appearances rather than formal roles. He advised young players like Ja Morant to "be better than me," urging authenticity while cautioning against pitfalls. In BIG3 coaching, he mentored with tough love, drawing from his own trials. Social media became his pulpit, shouting out rising stars and sharing life lessons. This role suited his reflective phase, a shift from spotlight chaser to sage. Emotionally, it bridged the distance from his playing intensity, offering purpose in guiding the next generation. Culturally, it positioned him as an elder statesman, his Hampton roots informing advice on identity and expression. Preparations included business ventures like Reebok's executive spot, blending legacy with leadership. As he navigated retirement's quiet, this elder status grew, a natural evolution.

The emotional chasm between Iverson's electrifying playing years and retirement life yawned wide, a space filled with introspection and reevaluation. The highs—48-point Finals games, MVP chants—contrasted sharply with the lows of empty arenas and personal reckonings. He spoke of hitting "rock bottom" post-divorce and financial whispers, moments that forced deep self-assessment. Family anchored him, his daughter's recovery a beacon amid turmoil. Culturally, this distance allowed perspective on his impact, turning pain into wisdom. Yet, the void lingered, the adrenaline rush irreplaceable. In quiet Hampton nights, he reflected on lost friends and mentors, mortality sharpening his gratitude. This emotional journey, from defiant star to contemplative figure, humanized his legend, grounding it in shared human frailty.

As Iverson settled into this new rhythm, the horizon hinted at greater affirmations—a Hall of Fame nod that would cement his place in basketball's pantheon, a canonization of his cultural revolutions, and the unfolding afterlife of an influence that refused to fade.

The Hall of Fame

In the spring of 2015, as the NBA playoffs unfolded without him, Allen Iverson received word that altered the trajectory of his post-playing life. The Naismith Memorial Basketball Hall of Fame had ruled him eligible for induction in 2016, a year earlier than some anticipated, dismissing his brief stint in Turkey as inconsequential to the retirement clock. Iverson had last suited up in the NBA in 2010, his career a whirlwind of brilliance and controversy that ended amid whispers of decline. Yet here was validation from the sport's highest sanctum, acknowledging that his three-year wait had sufficed. The announcement rippled through basketball circles, stirring memories of the undersized guard who had defied gravity and expectations. For Iverson, eligibility was more than procedural; it was a bridge to reckoning with a legacy that had polarized the league. Fans who had watched him cross over Michael Jordan as a rookie now pondered his place among immortals. The buildup began subtly, with podcasts and columns revisiting his MVP season in 2001, when he dragged a scrappy Philadelphia 76ers squad to the Finals. Whispers grew into debates: Was Iverson a first-ballot lock? His scoring titles, All-Star nods, and steals leadership screamed yes, but detractors pointed to efficiency metrics and ringless fingers. As summer turned to fall, anticipation swelled, fueled by Iverson's own reflections in interviews, where he spoke of gratitude without regret, hinting at the emotional weight of this honor. The Hall's decision ignited a collective pause, forcing the basketball world to confront the man who had reshaped its cultural fabric, one cornrow at a time.

By late 2015, the public anticipation for Iverson's potential enshrinement had evolved into a palpable emotional crescendo, as if the sport itself was exhaling after years of holding its breath. Social media buzzed with throwback clips of his ankle-breaking crossovers and defiant press conferences, users tagging #AIHOF in posts that blended nostalgia with reverence. In Philadelphia, where Iverson's No. 3 jersey still dotted the stands at Wells Fargo Center, fans organized watch parties for the announcement, their chants of "MVP" echoing from bars to barbershops. Nationally, the buildup mirrored a family reunion, with former teammates like Aaron McKie sharing stories of Iverson's unyielding work ethic behind closed doors. The emotional undercurrent was undeniable—here was a player who had embodied resilience, rising from a Hampton, Virginia, jail cell to NBA stardom, only to face scrutiny for his authenticity. As April 2016 approached, the date of the official class reveal, tension mounted. Would the honors committee, with its 24 voters needing 18 affirmations, recognize Iverson's intangibles? Leaks suggested a stacked class including Shaquille O'Neal and Yao Ming, heightening the drama. Iverson himself remained stoic in public, but those close to him noted a quiet introspection, as if this moment forced him to revisit the trials that forged him. The anticipation wasn't just about basketball; it was a cultural referendum on a figure who had challenged the league's buttoned-up image, making his induction feel like a long-overdue apology from the establishment.

Media retrospectives flooded the airwaves and pages in the months leading to the announcement, sharpening Iverson's legacy into a multifaceted gem that gleamed with both triumph and tumult. ESPN aired specials dissecting his career arc, from the 1996 draft where he was selected first overall by the Sixers, to his iconic step-over of Tyronn Lue in the 2001 Finals. Writers like Marc Stein and

Howard Beck penned essays exploring how Iverson's hip-hop-infused style—tattoos, baggy shorts, and arm sleeves—had initially alienated league executives but ultimately democratized the NBA's aesthetic. Documentaries revisited the 2002 "practice" rant, reframing it not as petulance but as raw honesty from a player burdened by expectations. NBA.com compiled stats highlighting his four scoring titles and three steals crowns, while podcasts like "The Lowe Post" debated his efficiency in an analytics era, concluding that his heart outweighed any spreadsheet. These pieces didn't shy from the shadows: the trades, the coaching clashes, the off-court headlines. Yet they converged on a narrative of revolution, portraying Iverson as the bridge between Michael Jordan's polished era and the expressive freedom of today's stars. In Philadelphia Inquirer columns, journalists like Mike Sielski evoked the city's blue-collar ethos, crediting Iverson for galvanizing a fanbase during lean years. The retrospectives built a monument to his influence, transforming scattered memories into a cohesive testament, ensuring that by induction time, his legacy stood not as divisive but as indispensable to the sport's evolution.

As the April 4, 2016, announcement neared, fan excitement reached fever pitch, manifesting in ways that underscored Iverson's enduring hold on the collective imagination. Online forums like Reddit's r/NBA exploded with threads predicting his enshrinement, users sharing personal anecdotes of mimicking his crossover in driveway games or adopting his sleeve as a middle-school fashion statement. In Hampton, his hometown organized a community viewing event, where elders recounted watching young Allen dazzle on local courts, blending football agility with basketball flair. Philadelphia fans, ever loyal, launched petitions for a statue outside the arena, their social media campaigns amassing thousands of signatures overnight. Globally, international admirers from China to Europe posted tribute videos, dubbing Iverson "The Answer" in multiple languages, a nod to his Reebok moniker. The excitement wasn't confined to digital spaces; merchandise sales spiked, with vintage jerseys flying off shelves. At All-Star Weekend in Toronto earlier that year, Iverson's appearance drew thunderous ovations, fans chanting his name as if he were still suiting up. This groundswell reflected more than nostalgia—it was a celebration of authenticity in an increasingly corporate league. As the day arrived, bars in Philly overflowed with patrons in No. 3 gear, their cheers erupting when his name was called alongside O'Neal and Ming. The moment crystallized fan devotion, proving Iverson's impact transcended stats, embedding him in the hearts of those who saw themselves in his unapologetic grit.

With Iverson's eligibility confirmed and his induction sealed, the NBA as an institution began a profound reevaluation of his entire career arc, acknowledging the layers beneath the headlines. League officials, once wary of his rebellious image, now highlighted his statistical dominance: 26.7 points per game lifetime, 11 All-Star selections, and a Rookie of the Year award. Commissioner Adam Silver, in statements, praised Iverson's role in globalizing the game, noting how his fearless drives inspired a new generation of guards. Analysts revisited his 2001 MVP campaign, where he averaged 31.1 points and led the Sixers to 56 wins, framing it as a masterclass in carrying a franchise. Even critics softened, admitting that his efficiency dips were offset by the defensive attention he drew, often facing double-teams that no metric could fully capture. The reevaluation extended to his off-court influence, with NBA executives crediting him for loosening dress codes and embracing urban culture, paving the way for today's tattooed, expressive athletes. In boardrooms, discussions turned to his resilience—overcoming a high school conviction, navigating trades to Denver and Detroit, and enduring media scrutiny without breaking. This holistic view repositioned Iverson not as a flawed talent but as a transformative force, whose arc from prodigy to pariah to legend mirrored the league's own maturation. By September, as the ceremony loomed, the NBA had woven him into its narrative fabric, celebrating the very qualities it once sought to tame.

The symbolism of Iverson entering the Hall of Fame resonated like a thunderclap, representing the ultimate vindication for a player who had waged war against conformity. At 6 feet and 165 pounds, he embodied the underdog, proving that heart could eclipse height in a giants' game. His induction symbolized the NBA's embrace of diversity, honoring a Black man from humble roots who infused the league with hip-hop's rhythm and rebellion. Tattoos once deemed thuggish now stood as badges of authenticity, his cornrows a statement against assimilation. For the sport, it marked a shift from Jordan's corporate polish to a more inclusive era, where players like LeBron James and Stephen Curry could express individuality without apology. Culturally, Iverson's enshrinement affirmed the Black experience in America—overcoming systemic barriers, from his wrongful imprisonment to league dress code battles. It symbolized redemption, turning "practice" memes into emblems of passion. For fans of color, it was a beacon, validating their heroes amid a league grappling with racial dynamics. Globally, it highlighted basketball's crossover appeal, with Iverson's style influencing fashion and music worldwide. As the Hall's doors opened to him, it wasn't just personal triumph; it was a monumental acknowledgment that revolution could coexist with reverence, forever altering the pantheon's silhouette.

On September 9, 2016, in Springfield, Massachusetts, the Naismith Memorial Basketball Hall of Fame induction ceremony unfolded under a canopy of lights, the Symphony Hall stage a shrine to hoops immortality. Iverson arrived fashionably late to the jacket presentation the day before, true to his maverick form, but on this night, he was punctual, clad in a sharp black suit that nodded to his streetwise roots. The visuals were poignant: orange-and-black banners for the class, spotlights casting long shadows as inductees like O'Neal and Ming towered nearby. When Iverson's turn came, introduced by Larry Brown, Julius Erving, and John Thompson, the crowd—a mix of suits, jerseys, and tear-streaked faces—erupted. His 31-minute speech was a tapestry of emotion, voice cracking as he thanked God for blessings amid no regrets. He evoked laughter recalling his mother's drag to practice, then sobs honoring deceased loved ones like Huddy Combs. The audience hung on every word, Philly fans in the balcony chanting "MVP" when he mentioned them, their roars drowning the hall. Reactions were visceral: O'Neal grinned at Iverson's "practice" quip, while Ming nodded knowingly. Tears flowed freely, from Iverson wiping his eyes to family members in the front row. The ceremony's climax saw him unveil his plaque, the moment frozen in flashes, emotions raw and unfiltered, a monumental tribute to a career that had always worn its heart on its sleeve.

Iverson's presence on that stage stood as a cultural milestone, a beacon illuminating the intersection of sport, identity, and rebellion. There he was, the kid from the projects, sharing the spotlight with giants, his slight frame amplified by the weight of history. It marked the NBA's formal acceptance of Black cultural expression, his tattoos and braids no longer outliers but emblems of progress. For generations raised on his highlights, it was validation that authenticity could conquer criticism, his journey from vilified to venerated echoing broader societal shifts. The milestone extended beyond basketball; it affirmed hip-hop's infiltration of mainstream America, Iverson the conduit who made cornrows cool in boardrooms. Young players watching saw possibility—Russell Westbrook's flair, Kyrie Irving's handles—traced back to this night. Emotionally, it was reverent, Iverson's humility contrasting his defiant past, a man at peace with his path. The hall, once a bastion of traditionalism, now housed a revolutionary, symbolizing the sport's evolution toward inclusivity. Reactions poured in real-time: social media alight with #AIHOF, fans hailing it as a win for the culture. This wasn't just enshrinement; it was a monumental pivot, etching Iverson's imprint into the annals as the architect of a freer, more vibrant game.

Players across generations responded to Iverson's induction with a chorus of admiration, their tributes underscoring his intergenerational bridge. Michael Jordan, his idol and victim of that famous crossover, sent a video message, congratulating "The Answer" with a warm embrace of respect. LeBron James tweeted immediately, calling Iverson "a pioneer who changed the game forever," reflecting on how AI's fearlessness inspired his own career. Veterans like Kobe Bryant, who had battled him in the Finals, praised his competitiveness, noting in interviews that Iverson's heart made him unbeatable on any given night. Younger stars like Stephen Curry lauded his scoring prowess, admitting to studying AI's footwork in youth leagues. Chris Paul, presenting at the ceremony, shared stories of emulating Iverson's handles, while Dwyane Wade later chose him as an inductor for his own Hall entry, citing forgotten impacts. Even rivals like Shaquille O'Neal, sharing the stage, joked about AI's "practice" rant before earnestly acknowledging his dominance. The responses weren't mere platitudes; they revealed a reevaluation, with analytics skeptics like Kevin Durant defending Iverson's efficiency in context. From legends to rookies, the outpouring was monumental, a collective nod to a player whose style and substance had redefined guard play, fostering a league where individuality thrived.

In Philadelphia, the community's reaction to Iverson's Hall of Fame honor was a seismic outpouring of pride, as if the city itself had been inducted. Streets buzzed with celebrations, from South Philly rowhouses to North Philly corners, where murals of AI already adorned walls. The 76ers organization hosted a watch party at the arena, fans in retro jerseys erupting when his speech aired, chanting "Thank you, Allen" in unison. Local media like the Inquirer ran front-page spreads, residents sharing tales of how Iverson's grit mirrored their own blue-collar ethos. Barbershops debated his legacy over fades, elders recalling his 2001 Finals run as the last true glory. The emotional depth was profound—tears in sports bars as he thanked Philly fans, acknowledging their unwavering support through trials. Community leaders hailed it as validation for the city's underdogs, with youth programs invoking AI's story to inspire kids. Even casual observers felt the weight; his induction symbolized Philly's resilience, a town that loved its flawed heroes. Reactions extended to gestures: the team retired his jersey anew in spirit, fans petitioning for a statue that would come years later. This wasn't fleeting joy; it was reverent affirmation, cementing Iverson as Philadelphia's eternal son, his enshrinement a monumental chapter in the city's sports lore.

The Black community's reaction to Iverson's induction carried a profound historical weight, viewing it as a triumph over systemic odds that had long shadowed athletes of color. From barbershops in Harlem to community centers in Atlanta, conversations framed AI as a symbol of unyielding Black excellence, his journey from wrongful incarceration to Hall immortality a narrative of redemption. Publications like The Root and Andscape ran essays celebrating his embrace of Black culture—cornrows, tattoos, hip-hop affiliations—once criticized but now canonized. Emotional responses poured forth: elders saw echoes of Muhammad Ali's defiance, while youth credited him for normalizing expressions of Black identity in sports. In Hampton, his Virginia roots, block parties erupted, residents honoring the local boy who made good despite the odds. Nationally, figures like Jesse Jackson praised Iverson's authenticity, noting how he challenged the NBA's assimilation pressures. The milestone resonated deeply, validating struggles against racial profiling and media bias that Iverson had endured. Tears flowed in living rooms as his speech thanked fallen friends, evoking communal loss. This enshrinement wasn't just personal; it was monumental for Black America, affirming that cultural revolutionaries could claim their place in history, inspiring a new wave to carry the torch with pride.

The hip-hop world and crossover culture embraced Iverson's Hall moment with fervent enthusiasm, recognizing it as coronation for their ambassador in the NBA. Artists like Jadakiss and Redman, whom Iverson thanked in his speech, posted tributes on Instagram, hailing him as the bridge between beats and baselines. Tupac and Biggie, invoked posthumously, symbolized AI's deep ties to the genre—his du-rags and chains once scandalous now iconic. Hip-hop media like Vibe and Complex ran features on his influence, crediting him for merging streetwear with athletic gear, spawning trends like arm sleeves that rappers adopted onstage. Emotional reactions came from peers: Post Malone's

"White Iverson" track surged in streams, the artist tweeting gratitude for the nod. Snoop Dogg called it "real recognize real," while Jay-Z referenced AI in lyrics as a cultural shifter. Crossover elements shone: fashion designers cited his Reebok line as pioneering athlete-endorsed street style. The moment validated hip-hop's infiltration of mainstream sports, with AI's induction a monumental fusion point. Communities celebrated with mixtapes blending his highlights with '90s tracks, affirming his role in democratizing culture. This embrace wasn't superficial; it was reverent, solidifying Iverson as the eternal link between hardwood and hood.

For Iverson personally, the Hall of Fame honor meant a profound closure, a divine affirmation of a life lived without apology. In interviews post-announcement, he reflected on it as God's blessing, erasing regrets from a career marked by highs like the 2001 MVP and lows like trades and scrutiny. It validated his sacrifices—nights away from family, battles with coaches—turning them into stepping stones. Emotionally, it was cathartic; his speech revealed vulnerability, tears for his mother who forced him into basketball, gratitude for Coach Thompson who saved him post-high school ordeal. Personally, it meant legacy for his children, showing them resilience pays off. Iverson spoke of idolizing Jordan, how crossing him felt surreal, now sharing the Hall with him. The honor mended wounds from media portrayals as troublesome, affirming his heart over headlines. In quiet moments, friends noted his humility, the weight lifting as he accepted this as proof of impact. Monumentally, it was redemption, allowing him to stand tall, no longer the rebel but the revered, a personal pinnacle that healed old scars.

Inducting Iverson validated his cultural revolution, enshrining the very disruptions that once threatened his standing. The NBA, which had imposed dress codes in 2005 partly in response to his style, now celebrated it as innovative. His induction affirmed that challenging norms—infusing hip-hop into the league, prioritizing authenticity over assimilation—could redefine an institution. Analysts noted how his playstyle liberated guards, his off-court persona empowering Black athletes to embrace heritage. The honor validated his impact on diversity, making the Hall more representative of the sport's urban roots. Emotionally, it was monumental, a league admitting that Iverson's "practice" passion and cultural flair were assets, not liabilities. For society, it underscored progress, his story a blueprint for overcoming bias. This validation wasn't token; it was reverent, cementing his revolution as essential to basketball's growth.

Yet even as the hype settled in Springfield, Iverson's story extended beyond the plaque, hinting at a vibrant afterlife where his imprint on culture, fashion, and the next generation would endure eternally, shaping worlds far removed from the court.

The Cultural Icon

In the pantheon of American sports heroes, few figures have undergone a metamorphosis as profound as Allen Iverson's. From a dazzling NBA star whose on-court brilliance captivated arenas in the late 1990s and early 2000s, Iverson ascended to legend status through his unyielding defiance and raw talent, only to transcend into something far more ethereal: a symbol. This transformation was not merely a product of his statistics—though his scoring titles and MVP award in 2001 etched him into basketball lore—but of his embodiment of rebellion against the sanitized expectations of professional athletics. Iverson's journey from star to legend began with his crossover dribble, a move that symbolized agility and unpredictability, mirroring his life's narrative of overcoming poverty, incarceration, and racial scrutiny. As legend, he represented the underdog's triumph, leading the Philadelphia 76ers to the 2001 NBA Finals against insurmountable odds. Yet, as symbol, Iverson became an archetype of authenticity, his cornrows and tattoos serving as visual manifestos against conformity.

This evolution reflects a psychological shift in cultural memory: Iverson is no longer just remembered for games won or lost, but for the emotional resonance of his persona, a beacon for those who feel marginalized. His image, frozen in iconic photographs of him stepping over Tyronn Lue, encapsulates influence that extends beyond sports, into the realms of identity and self-expression. Symbolism here is key; Iverson stands as a psychological anchor for generations grappling with societal pressures, his story a reminder that vulnerability and defiance can coexist in greatness. This symbolic stature ensures his legacy endures, not as a relic, but as a living force shaping how we perceive heroism in the modern era.

Today, conversations about Allen Iverson pulse with a mix of nostalgia and reverence, often framed as tributes to a cultural revolutionary rather than a retired athlete. In podcasts, social media threads, and barbershop debates, people invoke "AI" not for his points per game, but for his unapologetic embrace of Black urban culture amid a league that once sought to suppress it. Fans and analysts alike discuss him as the progenitor of the "realness" ethos in sports, where authenticity trumps polish. For instance, when contemporary players face criticism for their style or off-court antics, Iverson's name surfaces as a benchmark: "He's like AI, keeping it 100." This discourse reveals a psychological undercurrent, where memory of Iverson's battles—with coaches, commissioners, and public opinion—serves as catharsis for ongoing struggles against systemic conformity. His influence permeates think pieces in outlets like The Ringer or ESPN, portraying him as a symbol of resilience, his "practice" rant dissected not for petulance but for its raw honesty about the grind of stardom. Globally, in places like China or Europe where NBA fandom thrives, Iverson is talked about as an icon of individualism, his tattoos and braids inspiring tattoos and braids on fans who've never seen him play live. This contemporary dialogue blends admiration with introspection, questioning how sports culture has evolved since his era, and crediting him with paving the way for players to express their full selves without apology. Emotionally, these talks evoke a powerful sense of loss and gratitude, as if Iverson's story mirrors personal journeys of self-assertion.

Beyond the hardwood, Allen Iverson's global influence radiates like a cultural shockwave, touching lives far removed from basketball courts. In international markets, particularly Asia and Africa, Iverson emerged as a symbol of American cool, his Reebok sneakers and jerseys becoming staples in streetwear scenes from Tokyo to Johannesburg. This transcendence stems from his image as the ultimate underdog, a narrative that resonates universally in societies valuing perseverance amid adversity. Psychologically, Iverson represents the triumph of the individual spirit over institutional barriers, inspiring entrepreneurs, artists, and activists who see in him a blueprint for defying norms. His influence on global youth culture is evident in how his aesthetic—sleeveless jerseys, arm sleeves—has been adopted in soccer fields and skate parks worldwide, symbolizing freedom from traditional athletic decorum. Memory plays a role here; archival footage of his crossovers circulates on platforms like TikTok, introducing new generations to his legend and embedding his symbolism in digital folklore. In regions grappling with globalization, Iverson stands as a bridge between American hip-hop and local expressions, his story fostering cross-cultural dialogues on identity. This outside-basketball impact underscores his role as a psychological touchstone, where influence isn't measured in endorsements but in the subtle ways he altered perceptions of what a hero looks like—tattooed, braided, and unbreakable.

Allen Iverson's imprint on athlete identity and freedom of expression remains one of his most enduring legacies, reshaping how sports figures navigate their public selves. In an era when the NBA enforced dress codes to curb "thug" imagery, Iverson's refusal to conform—opting for baggy jeans and do-rags over suits—became a manifesto for personal liberty. This stance influenced a psychological shift among athletes, encouraging them to view their identities as integral to their performance, not liabilities. His symbolism as the "Answer" extended to answering back against suppression, empowering players to express cultural roots without fear of backlash.

Today, this freedom manifests in athletes like LeBron James or Russell Westbrook, who credit Iverson with normalizing vulnerability and style as strengths. The cultural memory of Iverson's press conferences, where he bared his soul, blends with images of his on-court ferocity, creating a holistic influence that promotes emotional authenticity. By challenging the league's conservative ethos, Iverson symbolized the fight for self-definition, his tattoos narrating stories of struggle that athletes now proudly display. This evolution in athlete identity fosters a broader symbolism: sports as a canvas for personal narrative, where expression isn't rebellion but essence.

Iverson's symbiosis with hip-hop culture elevated him to a pantheon where sports and music intertwined, forever altering both landscapes. As a figure who embodied the grit of East Coast rap—drawing parallels to artists like Jay-Z and DMX—his presence in lyrics and videos symbolized the merger of athletic prowess with street credibility. Rappers referenced his crossover in bars about outmaneuvering life's obstacles, while Iverson's own forays into music, like his unreleased album, blurred boundaries between fields. This influence stemmed from his authentic roots in Hampton, Virginia's hip-hop scene, where beats and ball-handling shared rhythmic synergy. Psychologically, Iverson represented the validation of urban narratives in mainstream arenas, his image inspiring producers to sample his highlights in tracks. Memory of his Reebok commercials, scored to hip-hop anthems, evokes a powerful nostalgia for an era when athletes could be cultural curators. Symbolically, he became the bridge for hip-hop's global export, his style influencing artists worldwide to adopt basketball motifs in their aesthetics.

The ripple effects of Iverson's fashion choices—cornrows, tattoos, oversized jerseys—revolutionized aesthetics in sports and beyond, embedding his DNA into everyday style. His cornrows, once deemed unprofessional, became symbols of cultural pride, influencing hairstyles from schoolyards to runways. Tattoos, previously taboo in the NBA, transformed under Iverson's influence into canvases of personal history, with his ink telling tales of loyalty and loss. This aesthetic shift blended psychology and image, as his look empowered individuals to wear their stories visibly, challenging norms of conformity. In fashion, brands like Nike and Adidas drew from his streetwear ethos, creating lines that celebrated urban flair. Memory of Iverson's arm sleeve, born from necessity but evolving into iconography, stirs emotional connections to rebellion. Symbolically, his influence on aesthetics promotes individuality, his persona a blueprint for blending grit with glamour.

Modern NBA players carry traces of Iverson's essence, embodying his fearless approach in ways that honor his pioneering spirit. Stars like Kyrie Irving or Ja Morant channel his crossover artistry and unfiltered personality, their tattoos and braids echoing Iverson's visual defiance. This inheritance reflects a psychological continuum, where Iverson's battles for expression paved the way for today's athletes to prioritize mental health and authenticity. Influence here is profound; players cite his MVP season as inspiration for playing through pain, symbolizing resilience. Cultural memory of his Finals run infuses current narratives, with young guards adopting his quickness as a nod to his legend. Image-wise, Iverson's symbolism lives in the league's relaxed dress code, allowing players to showcase personal style without repercussion.

Fans' emotional bonds to Iverson's narrative run deep, rooted in his story's universal themes of redemption and defiance. For many, especially in Philadelphia, he symbolizes the city's blue-collar ethos, his underdog journey mirroring personal struggles against odds. This attachment blends memory and psychology, with fans recounting his games as pivotal life moments, evoking tears and triumph. Influence extends to global admirers who see in him a symbol of hope, his vulnerabilities making him relatable. Symbolically, Iverson represents the human side of stardom, fostering communities where his story inspires overcoming adversity.

Iverson fundamentally altered sports culture's embrace of authenticity, shifting from performative perfection to genuine selfhood. Before him, athletes were expected to embody stoic ideals; his raw pressers and on-court passion symbolized a break, encouraging leagues to value realness. This change has psychological ramifications, reducing stigma around emotional expression in sports. Memory of his "practice" moment now symbolizes honesty over facade, influencing how authenticity is prized in endorsements and media. Culturally, Iverson's impact promotes a symbolism where flaws enhance legacy, reshaping fan expectations.

Within Black culture, Iverson holds sacred meaning as a symbol of unyielding pride amid systemic challenges. His rise from incarceration to stardom embodies the resilience narrative central to Black American experiences, his cornrows and tattoos affirming cultural aesthetics against assimilation pressures. Psychologically, he represents validation, his influence inspiring Black youth to embrace heritage. Memory of his community ties evokes emotional power, symbolizing collective triumph. In broader discourse, Iverson's persona blends influence and symbolism, reinforcing Black excellence on one's terms.

Iverson's legacy profoundly shaped social views on individuality, normalizing deviation from norms in a conformity-driven world. His refusal to dilute his identity symbolized the value of uniqueness, influencing attitudes toward personal expression in workplaces and schools. Psychologically, this fosters self-acceptance, with his story as a touchstone for those feeling othered. Cultural memory of his defiance blends with images of his triumphs, promoting a symbolism where individuality equals strength. This influence extends to policy shifts, like relaxed dress codes, reflecting broader acceptance.

In the struggle for cultural representation, Iverson emerged as a frontline warrior, his visibility challenging stereotypes and demanding inclusion. By bringing hip-hop elements into the NBA, he symbolized the push for diverse narratives, influencing media to portray multifaceted Black athletes. Psychologically, this role empowered marginalized voices, his influence creating space for authentic stories. Memory of his endorsements evokes pride, symbolizing representation's power. Globally, Iverson's fight resonates, blending culture and symbolism in ongoing equity battles.

Iverson's narrative echoes across generations, from Gen X fans who witnessed his prime to Gen Z discovering him via highlights. This resonance stems from its timeless themes of grit and authenticity, psychologically bridging eras through shared human struggles. Influence on youth culture persists, with his symbolism inspiring new waves of expression. Memory blends with image, creating an emotional continuum where his story feels eternally relevant.

The mythos surrounding Iverson endures as a tapestry of legend and lore, where facts intertwine with symbolism to form an immortal persona. Tales of his practice habits or off-court life amplify his image as the ultimate rebel, psychologically captivating audiences with archetypal heroism. This mythos influences cultural storytelling, his narrative a symbol for underdog epics. Emotionally powerful, it evokes a sense of wonder, blending memory and influence in perpetual reverence.

As a blueprint for the modern athlete, Iverson laid the foundation for integrating culture, personality, and performance seamlessly. Today's stars—from tattooed guards to socially conscious forwards—embody his DNA, symbolizing freedom in expression and resilience. This influence reshapes athlete psychology, prioritizing holistic identity. Memory of his era informs current dynamics, his symbolism a guiding force.

Epilogue — The Legacy of 3

In the quiet aftermath of a storm that once raged across hardwood courts and cultural landscapes, the legacy of Allen Iverson endures like an echo that refuses to fade. From the gritty streets of Hampton, Virginia, where a young boy named Allen learned to dribble through adversity, to the blinding lights of NBA arenas where he became a global icon, Iverson's journey was never a straight path but a labyrinth of triumphs and trials. Born into a world of poverty and peril, he carried the weight of his origins like a badge of honor, transforming personal pain into public performance. His crossover dribble wasn't just a move; it was a metaphor for evading expectations, slipping past defenders both on and off the court. As he rose from high school phenom to Georgetown standout, and then to the Philadelphia 76ers' savior, Iverson reshaped not only games but generations. He arrived in the league in 1996, a 6-foot underdog with cornrows and tattoos that screamed defiance, challenging the polished facade of professional sports. His story arc—from jail time in his youth to MVP honors in 2001—mirrored the American dream twisted through the prism of reality, where success demanded not conformity but unyielding authenticity. Today, long after his retirement in 2013, Iverson's narrative inspires artists, athletes, and everyday rebels who see in him a blueprint for rising against the odds. His path from Hampton's shadows to the Hall of Fame in 2016 encapsulates the essence of "3": the number on his jersey, the symbol of his stature, and the emblem of a movement that transcended basketball.

Revisiting the core themes that defined Iverson's era, one finds culture intertwined with rebellion, authenticity forged in the fires of identity. He was the bridge between hip-hop's raw energy and the NBA's corporate sheen, wearing baggy shorts and arm sleeves that became uniforms for a new wave of expression. Rebellion wasn't mere posturing for Iverson; it was survival, a refusal to dilute his Black identity for acceptance in a league dominated by traditional norms. He spoke truth to power, whether in press conferences decrying practice or in his unapologetic embrace of street culture. Authenticity radiated from his every pore—those cornrows weren't fashion; they were roots, connecting him to communities long marginalized. Identity, for Iverson, was fluid yet fierce, a blend of vulnerability and valor that invited fans to see themselves in his struggles. He didn't hide his scars; he inked them on his skin, turning personal history into public art. This interplay of themes created a cultural shift, where sports stars could be flawed heroes rather than infallible idols. Iverson's influence seeped into music, fashion, and film, inspiring figures like Lil Wayne and designers who echoed his aesthetic. In an age of curated images, his rawness reminded us that true culture blooms from the cracks of conformity, that rebellion fuels progress, and that authenticity is the ultimate identity. "3" thus evolved from a jersey digit to a manifesto, urging all to claim their space without apology.

Yet Iverson's sway extends far beyond the boundaries of basketball, infiltrating realms where perseverance meets societal change. In music, his ethos lives in tracks that sample his interviews, turning his words into anthems of grit. Fashion houses draw from his style, with sneakers and apparel lines paying homage to the crossover king who made urban wear mainstream. Even in social justice movements, Iverson's legacy whispers of resistance, his life a testament to challenging systemic barriers. He showed that influence isn't measured in championships—though he dragged the 76ers to the 2001 Finals against all odds—but in the lives touched by his example. Beyond the court, "3" symbolizes a broader movement: the democratization of cool, where kids from forgotten neighborhoods dream big without shedding their essence. His story resonates in boardrooms and barrios alike, proving that vulnerability can be a superpower. Iverson's off-court battles—with finances, addictions, and public scrutiny—didn't diminish his impact; they amplified it, humanizing success in a world obsessed with perfection. Today, as athletes like Kyrie Irving or Ja Morant channel his spirit, Iverson's reach proves timeless, a force that molds not just games but global conversations on race, class, and self-expression. His legacy endures because it speaks to the universal quest for meaning, turning personal rebellion into collective empowerment.

The emotional power of Iverson's imperfections and vulnerabilities lies at the heart of his enduring appeal, a raw humanity that draws us closer rather than pushing us away. He was no saint; his career was punctuated by controversies—missed practices, casino nights, and legal entanglements that painted him as the anti-hero. Yet these flaws didn't erode his stature; they built it, revealing a man who wore his heart on his sleeve, literally and figuratively. Vulnerability shimmered in his tearful retirements and comebacks, in the way he spoke of his mother's sacrifices or his own fears. Imperfections became his armor, shielding him from the facade of invincibility that plagues many icons. Fans connected not despite his stumbles but because of them, seeing reflections of their own struggles in his falls and rises. This emotional resonance turned Iverson into a mirror for the marginalized, a figure who validated pain as part of the path to glory. His 2001 MVP speech, laced with gratitude amid chaos, captured this duality: triumph born from turmoil. In a polished world, his unfiltered soul evoked empathy, forging bonds that outlast statistics. "3" thus embodies the beauty of brokenness, where vulnerabilities fuel connection and imperfections inspire resilience. Iverson's story teaches that true strength emerges from embracing the fractures, turning personal wounds into wellsprings of communal healing.

Through it all, "3" transformed into a profound symbol of perseverance, expression, and truth, a beacon for those navigating life's hard ways. Perseverance defined Iverson's every step—from overcoming a wrongful conviction in his teens to battling injuries that would fell lesser athletes. He played through pain, averaging over 40 minutes per game in his prime, his small frame defying giants. Expression flowed from his artistry on the court, where crossovers and finger rolls were poetry in motion, and off it, where he championed individuality against league dress codes. Truth was his compass, unvarnished and unyielding, whether admitting faults or defending his culture. "3" became shorthand for this triad: the dogged pursuit of dreams, the bold voicing of self, and the honest reckoning with reality. It represents the underdog's roar, the artist's canvas, the truth-teller's stand. In Iverson's hands, a simple number evolved into a movement, inspiring tattoos, chants, and lifestyles that echo his ethos. Perseverance in the face of doubt, expression amid suppression, truth over pretense—these are the pillars of "3," a symbol that outlives its bearer, guiding future generations toward authentic victory.

Iverson remains beloved across generations because his essence bridges eras, speaking to the young and old with equal fervor. Millennials remember him as the rebel who shattered NBA norms, while Gen Z discovers him through viral clips and documentaries, drawn to his unapologetic vibe in an era of social media scrutiny. Elders admire his work ethic, forged in an analog world, while kids emulate his swagger on playgrounds worldwide.

This cross-generational love stems from his relatability: he was everyman and superman, flawed yet phenomenal. Retirees in Hampton share stories of his local roots, while global fans in Asia or Europe wear his jerseys as talismans of tenacity. His induction into the Hall of Fame solidified this adoration, but it's the intangible—his heart—that cements it. Iverson's philanthropy, quiet acts of kindness, and candid reflections in later years deepened the bond, showing growth without losing edge. Beloved not for perfection but for passion, he unites disparate souls in admiration. "3" fosters this timeless affection, a cultural thread weaving through ages, reminding all that heroes are human, and love endures through authenticity.

The cultural revolution Iverson sparked reshaped sports and society, igniting a fire that still burns brightly. He dismantled barriers, paving the way for tattooed athletes and hip-hop integrations that now define the NBA. His defiance against dress codes in 2005 foreshadowed broader acceptance of diversity, influencing leagues to embrace cultural pluralism. Society felt the ripple: fashion trends exploded with AI-inspired gear, music videos featured his highlights, and conversations on Black excellence amplified. This revolution wasn't planned; it was organic, born from one man's refusal to conform. Iverson's impact challenged stereotypes, empowering youth to own their narratives in a world quick to judge. From boardrooms adopting casual attire to schools fostering self-expression, his revolution permeates. "3" ignited this shift, turning individual rebellion into societal evolution, where authenticity trumps assimilation.

In the permanence of his imprint, Iverson's legacy etches itself into the fabric of sports and society, an indelible mark that time cannot erase. Stadiums echo his name in chants, museums preserve his artifacts, and scholars dissect his influence on identity politics. His story endures in books, films, and folklore, a testament to how one life can alter trajectories. Sports evolved because of him—more inclusive, expressive, real—while society grapples with the truths he unveiled about race and resilience. This permanence lies in the intangible: the spark he lit in countless hearts, urging them to live boldly. "3" stands as eternal proof that myths are made from men who dare to be movements.

And so, in the grand tapestry of human endeavor, "3" endures as a timeless cultural idea, forever embodying the hard-won harmony of struggle and splendor.

Sources & Further Reading

The research and narrative insights in *3 The Hard Way: How Allen Iverson Reshaped The Culture* were informed by a wide range of publicly available materials, historical records, broadcast interviews, and long-form journalism. All sources were used for contextual understanding only; no copyrighted text was reproduced.

Basketball Databases & Historical Records

- NBA.com: Official league archives and historical statistics
- Basketball-Reference.com: Game logs, season summaries, and player timelines
- Naismith Memorial Basketball Hall of Fame: Induction archives and career validations

Public Interviews & Broadcast Material

- Press conferences and televised interviews featuring Allen Iverson
- Nationally broadcast NBA media availability
- Hall of Fame ceremony broadcasts
- NBA TV and ESPN archival features

Documentaries & Long-Form Video Content

- Nationally aired Allen Iverson documentary retrospectives

- NBA-produced historical series and features
- Publicly available YouTube archival footage from official NBA partners

Sports Journalism & Cultural Analysis

- ESPN.com: Long-form features, player profiles, and retrospective essays
- The Undefeated / Andscape: Cultural and identity-focused reporting
- The Ringer: Player legacy evaluations and cultural commentary
- Complex Sports: Hip-hop and basketball crossover features
- Slam Magazine: Historical profiles and cover stories

General Cultural & Historical Context

- Publicly available reporting on hip-hop, Black cultural identity, and sports style evolution
- Academic work on athlete influence, cultural expression, and representation
- Public interviews with former players, coaches, and cultural commentators

This book synthesizes broadly known events, cultural narratives, and publicly accessible historical information to examine Allen Iverson's lasting impact on sports, culture, and identity.

www.ingramcontent.com/pod-product-compliance
Ingram Content Group UK Ltd.
Pitfield, Milton Keynes, MK11 3LW, UK
UKHW021036270726
13967UKWH00013B/2812

9 781970 85000(